The Observant Eye

To order additional copies, please contact us.
BookSurge, LLC
www.booksurge.com
1-866-308-6235
orders@booksurge.com

The Observant Eye

WT Subalusky

2006

The Observant Eye

TABLE OF CONTENTS

ABOUT THE AUTHOR AND OBSERVATIONS

I was standing off in the corner of the room, watching the activities around me, like the proverbial fly on the wall. In the middle of the room lay a middle-aged man. Several other people moved quickly about the room expressing worries over the man's obviously distended stomach. In walked a man in a mask and the worried murmurs quieted. The masked man took what appeared to be a knife and, without hesitation, sliced open the man's stomach. Instantly, like one of those surprise joke boxes loaded with a cloth covered spring that jumps out to frighten the unwary opener, the man's air-gorged intestines popped into the air. The masked man remarked on the cause of the condition of the intestines and quickly directed actions that would eliminate the intestinal blockage causing the problem. Within minutes, the condition was apparently under control.

I watched the above drama unfold as I stood in the corner of one of the operating rooms in a major hospital. My objective was to observe activities and suggest ways to improve patient safety. Following the above observation and several others, I made a number of recommendations. I am not a physician. In fact, I know no more about medical science than the interested person can acquire from laymen's medical books and the internet. I do, however, know a good bit of other information related to work in a complex and technical environment such as a hospital operating room. I know how a group of individuals performing a complex task can become more effective by working as a team, with each individual playing, and recognized to be playing, an important role. I have seen this on submarines and I have seen it in the control room crews of a commercial nuclear power plant. I know what "good" looks like in the exchange of information between individuals when the accuracy and completeness of that information is vital to the success of the information transfer, and in some cases, to the lives of those involved. I have seen this in the transfers of information between nuclear plant watch-standers. I know the techniques that individuals can use to reduce the likelihood of making a personnel error such as operating the wrong valve on a submarine, turning the wrong switch in an operating nuclear reactor, or administering the wrong medication to a patient. I know what a real focus on safety looks like, whether it's nuclear safety in an operating nuclear power plant, patient safety in a hospital, or personnel safety in any other hazardous environment. I know that the "picture" of performance of any organization is like the picture in a jigsaw puzzle. It does not reveal itself until all or most of the pieces have been identified and placed in their proper location. And I know that the most effective way to identify areas of performance that need attention -- to find and position those puzzle pieces that reveal the true performance picture -- is by observing people work.

Although my education is sound and certainly does not hamper my observation abilities, neither is it the basis for those abilities. I obtained a bachelor's degree in electrical engineering. My master's degree came shortly thereafter. The latter consisted of a cross-disciplinary advanced education in electrical engineering, mechanical engineering, and underwater acoustics. Both degrees were completed with enough academic success to warrant membership in several engineering-related honor societies. Subsequently, I completed advanced studies in nuclear engineering as well as graduated from the Harvard Business School's Advanced Management Program. Considered all together, I spent nearly ten years in formal education following high school. However, I recall that neither my schooling nor any of the readings associated with it even hinted at the use or importance of the skill of observing people work and its link to improving performance -- a skill I would subsequently learn is essential to the effective operation of any facility, organization, or even home.

My ability to evaluate organizations by observing people as they perform their day-to-day activities evolved through work experience that involved more than forty-five years and multiple careers. That experience included operating nuclear submarines, evaluating the performance of commercial nuclear generating stations, managing the generation of electrical power, teaching both technical and leadership topics, and conducting private consulting activities.

I had long seen the value of observing people work during my time in the nuclear field. However, I saw the potential value of applying it to a much broader spectrum of activities after I started my own consulting business and became sensitized to the performance problems and events occurring in other areas. Those areas encompassed the chemical industry, healthcare, and even government controlled evolutions such as emergency response and community evacuations. These areas were exhibiting the same types of problems that observations had long ago helped to resolve in the nuclear business. My thoughts were confirmed when I began performing assessments of patient safety in the healthcare community and had the opportunity to observe physicians, nurses, and other caregivers as they went about their activities in caring for patients. This, of course, was all with the back drop that almost 100,000 of these patients die unnecessarily each year as a result of preventable medical errors. In all of these fields, as with most others, understanding performance is critically important to improving that performance. The single most important thing I have learned over my career is that if you want to understand performance, you must observe people work -- observe their activities, their surroundings, and their management.

My foundation in the art of observation was built in the military. I spent twenty years in the U.S. submarine force, this time being equally divided between being an enlisted sailor or "rag hat" and subsequently a commissioned line officer on nuclear submarines. As an officer, I was proud to hold the unofficial title of "mustang," having first had ten years experience as an enlisted sailor. It was during my enlisted time, when I progressed through essentially all of the achievable enlisted ranks, that I had the opportunity to develop the experience of a hands-on worker. This opportunity allowed me to see, first hand, how important it is in observing to understand the perspectives of the working level as they apply to the issues of management. My experience as a rag hat allowed me to appreciate the problems of the worker. I was comfortable in the trenches -- where the wrenches turn, where the work gets done, where the rubber meets the road, and where one needs to go to see the fruits of management (good or bad) and their impact on the workers and their performance.

My time as a commissioned officer was no less valuable

in building on that foundation of an observer. Progressing from the most junior to the senior officer ranks, I had the opportunity to see the same kinds of issues I saw as a worker, but from the totally different perspective of a senior manager.

In essentially every military assignment I had, the ability to critically observe played a key role. Such was the case, even though the assignments varied so widely, from that of Controllerman on a diesel submarine, operating the levers that controlled the power which drove the sub through the deep darkness, to an instructor's role in the training of Navy nuclear operators, to an advisor on a surface ship hunting submarines below, to Chief Engineer on a state of the art nuclear submarine. The key message that was repeatedly reinforced in all of these activities was: observe the people work, pay attention to detail, expect to see only the highest of standards, and question anything that's out-of-the-ordinary.

Following my naval career, and probably to a large degree because of the habits I developed in observing people work and expecting only the highest of standards, I was employed by a private oversight organization that was just in its formative stages. In this new career, I had the opportunity to help in the development and implementation of an observation process -- a process in which highly experienced and specially trained people watch workers go about their daily activities, and then, based on the observations, provide an assessment of the organization's effectiveness. Performance assessment through observing activities would be a key part of my professional life for the next two decades. This fledgling company subsequently grew to become the most influential force in achieving the remarkable improvement record of the safety and reliability of commercial nuclear generating plants. For almost the next twenty years, I conducted performance assessments by observing the activities inside the complex and potentially hazardous environment of nuclear plants. I also periodically observed and assessed the performance of the related corporate organizations. Once again joining the company at the entry level as a reviewer, I progressed through the ranks to retire as a vice president of the company. The value of starting at the working level once more was reinforced, giving me a far better appreciation of the challenges of being a working-level reviewer than that of many of my colleagues in management. Among other assignments during my civilian career in assessment, I served as the Executive Director of the National Academy of Nuclear Training, responsible for assessing and guiding the training activities of essentially all of the nuclear workers in the U.S. It was this experience, coupled with the value placed on training imbued in me during my years in the nuclear submarine force, which allowed me to discover the value of observing training activities as part of the scope of almost any assessment. My civilian career also included holding executive level positions in several private companies, where I walked in the shoes of a line executive and gained an appreciation of what it is like to be on the observed side of assessment. As a senior executive responsible for the operation of a large electric power generating facility, the importance of critically observing became even more evident. I subsequently "retired" and soon started my own consulting business, again in the assessment area. I continued my strong focus on observing people work. During my civilian career in assessment, I have observed or led teams that observed the activities of hundreds of organizations, including every commercial nuclear generating site in the United States and several in other countries, a number of Department of Energy facilities, a wide range of hospitals, and numerous commercial enterprises where, as a customer, I continued to apply and benefit from my observation skills.

It is the above background that has made me such a fervent

believer in the value of observing people work -- a simple but powerful tool that can be used by anyone interested in evaluating and improving performance.

CHAPTER 1
WHY READ THIS BOOK

The shelves of uncountable numbers of book cases currently bend under the weight of a more than generous lot of management books. The information flows like a river of words and ideas, with a never ending supply of new (or more often, restated and recycled) thoughts and advice. Some of these word collections stick in the mainstream for a period of time, while others come and go quickly like fads in fashion. They all eventually move along in the stream to make room for the current of new ideas. Advice is provided on how to manage in periods of one minute, how to improve performance, how to communicate, how to involve the employees, how to conduct "crucial conversations," how to become great if you are already good. What they don't provide is important information on how to identify what needs the management attention that you will devote in that one minute; how to identify what performance to improve; how to know what you should be communicating about; how to know what issues the employees should be involved in resolving; how to know when performance indicates a need for one of those crucial conversations; how to objectively assess whether you are good and ready to move to great, or bad and needing to move to good. In short, how does someone really know what's going on in his or her organization, or business, or home? The answers to these questions are encompassed in this book.

Think about this: If you were wealthy enough to afford your own chauffer, would you let him drive you anywhere if you first concluded he couldn't see the road? What if he could see the road but had only a fuzzy view and could see some but not all of the things on the road? Or if he could see clearly but, for whatever reason, chose to look at only one side of the road? Of course you wouldn't, you say. But everyday, managers are allowed to steer organizations even though they aren't able to clearly see where that organization is, where it is headed, and the potholes and obstructions that lie on the road before it. A driver is required to take an eye exam before getting a license to drive a vehicle, but managers are rarely if ever examined on how well they see, through assessment, before being hired or put in charge with the license to drive an organization.

The simple analogy of driving a car is descriptive. If you want to get from point A to point B, your driving abilities allow you to get there by knowing how much gas to apply to the engine and how much braking or steering to apply. However, this is only the case if you can clearly see the road and your surroundings and know when and how much to do what. This element of "seeing the road" or assessment, in the management vernacular, is one of the least talked about attributes of management. It is a factor that is seldom if ever mentioned in such books as those referred to above. Yet assessment skills are among the weakest of the typical manager's abilities. The evidence of this weakness appears so frequently in the news media that, as a society, we tend to accept ignorance as an excuse. Newspapers, magazines, and television news are replete with examples of industry leaders pleading ignorance of what's going on in their organizations, and providing this as an excuse when problems occur in the companies they manage. Watch the news with this sensitivity and you will frequently see the lawyerly efforts that are oriented toward proving some executive faultless because he was unaware of what was happening within his organization. The follow-on question of why <u>didn't</u> he know what was going on is one not frequently enough asked.

Continuing with the car analogy -- if the vehicle (or organization) is a small one, like a car (or small company), the driver can do the assessment by himself. But if it is large, more like a cruise ship (or large company), then multiple people are involved in "watching" the route and causing the ship to follow the intended course. In the analogous large organization, the "captain" who, like the captain of a ship, can delegate authority but not ultimate responsibility, depends on other assets, such as line managers and oversight groups, to help "watch the road." It is the shortfalls in this watching or observing by the driver or captain and by these other groups, which I have witnessed for over forty years, that are the basis of this book. Oversight groups, such as Quality Assurance, Performance Assurance, or others, under whatever title flag they may fly, ironically are often among the weakest of the watchers.

With regularity, the news headlines remind readers that safety is deficient in a wide range of industries -- patient safety, mine safety, chemical safety, and farm safety, to name a few. Even in the nuclear industry, which has long focused on its piece of the safety pie -- nuclear safety -- and has made remarkable improvements over the last several decades, more needs to be done. So it is likely that the reader will be interested in improving safety. Yet in the following chapters I refer to improving "performance." To explain what at first appears to be a disconnect between what is needed and what is presented here, let me clarify what the difference is between "safety" and "performance". In a word, the difference is nothing. Safety is an integral part of performance. It is not conceptually possible to have "good performance" while simultaneously having poor safety. You can't boast with justified pride about all of the money you are making or all of the products or services you are providing, if at the same time you are injuring or killing people while doing it. Similarly, if you want to improve safety in an organization, you first need to take those actions that directly affect performance, such as changing the behaviors of people; getting line managers more involved with the workers; providing clear expectations that reflect high standards; ensuring the clarity of the policies; insisting that needed policies not only are developed, but implemented as well. These are the kinds of things needed to improve safety; these are as well the kinds of things needed to improve performance. Fundamental actions required to improve safety are inseparable from those required to improve performance in general. In the early 1980s, the nuclear industry started a concerted effort to improve the nuclear safety of its power plants. After two decades, it had achieved that goal and more. At the same time, the production figures of the industry improved from an average in the mid-sixty percent range to the current average in the mid ninety percent range. This was not a coincidence. Improvement in production performance is a positive, although not often expected, side effect of efforts to improve safety.

The subject matter of this book could serve a variety of professionals well. The typical corporate staff is one example. I have, on numerous occasions, led assessment teams in conducting performance reviews of large corporate organizations. Team objectives included determining what needed to be done differently by the corporate office in order to provide better support of the company's operating facilities -- where the product is produced; where the customer is dealt with; where the money is made or lost. The reviews were typically a week in length, and I religiously first visited the operating facilities, looking for performance issues that one would expect a corporate organization to be involved in helping to resolve. It was not unusual, after only a short way through one of these reviews, to realize that I knew considerably more about what was happening at the operating facilities and the issues they were facing than did the majority of the corporate staff. The irony was not lost on me that these were the people who at that very time were at the corporate office developing the policies and procedural direction that the facility staffs were expected to follow! A number of such experiences led me to conclude that corporate staffs are generally weak in assessment skills -- a topic rarely written about or discussed in management forums.

The usefulness herein is not limited to oversight personnel and corporate office staff. Any manager with responsibility for an organization or even an element of an organization, regardless of its size, can benefit from applying the concepts and techniques in this book. In fact, even though the terminology here is directed toward the position of a manager, every adult, in the course of his or her personal life, can apply and benefit from many of the concepts discussed here. After all, it would be hard to argue against the point that operating our homes in many respects is not unlike running a small business.

As a consultant I have been paid large sums of money to come into an organization and tell managers what their people are doing. This fact speaks volumes for the distance that many managers have yet to go in achieving a level of job performance at which they can truthfully say they are doing what they are getting paid to do. After all, a key part of any manager's job is assessing or observing, or watching the road.

The improvement guru, Deming, found that 85% of problems in an organization are due to "management systems." My personal experience with reviews performed at literally hundreds of organizations in several different fields has independently led me to the same conclusion; however, being less kind than Mr. Deming, I would not include the word "systems" in the proclamation. Take a look at the assessment plans or schedules at any organization -- if they exist -- and see how many reviews or observations are focused directly on the activities of managers. You will find few if any. The point is, most problems exist because managers are not aware of them. This in turn is primarily because managers are not observing. And no one knows managers are not observing because no one is observing the managers. The concepts and techniques described in this and the following chapters can help both the managers and those responsible for the managers "see the road" in front of them.

I cannot speak strongly enough in support of the heart of this book -- the value of observing and observing effectively. It is the only management tool that causes positive change not only by its use but even by its very existence. If a healthy and effective observation effort exists in any organization, people will do even more than they might ordinarily do to fix or preclude problems, improve performance, or upgrade conditions. They will be motivated at least in part by the desire to maintain their pride when others come to observe; to avoid the embarrassment of others identifying shortfalls in their area. It is ironic that such an important tool of management is among the least effectively used -- with a few exceptions.

THE NUCLEAR WAY AND THE OTHER WAY

I have told my wife on a number of occasions, and somewhat facetiously, if I am ever in urgent need of medical care, call 911 and have the ambulance take me to the nearest nuclear power plant. Why? Because hospitals worry me and nuclear plants don't. The plants won't have the best medical expertise in the world as many of our hospitals do. They won't have the medical equipment that so far surpasses that of any other place on earth as many of our hospitals do. The workers at those plants likely won't even have that special gift of caring that allows nurses and other caregivers to see through the ugliness of disease and to treat each patient as a special human being. But they also don't have the less-than-illustrious performance track record that hospitals have. Any set of statistics can be questioned, but the barrage of statistics and newspaper headlines that point to a medical crisis in healthcare performance is unavoidable. If even half of this information is anywhere close to accurate, we have a problem -- from a medical layman's perspective, a big problem.

A study by the Institute of Medicine (IOM) in 1999 concluded that as many as 98,000 people die each year as a result of preventable medical errors. Another study, which reanalyzed the same data as that used in the IOM study, concluded the number of deaths is closer to 195,000 every year. Preventable medical mistakes cost more lives each year than motor vehicle accidents, AIDS, breast cancer, diabetes, influenza, pneumonia, and Alzheimer's. One of our northern states recently implemented required reporting of those medical errors that are described as "likely to cause death or serious disability," and are defined by the medical community as events that "should never happen." In a one month period ending in late 2005, 103 of these events were reported. The events were tied to 12 patient deaths, 9 disabilities, 26 cases of leaving foreign objects in patients after surgery, and 16 cases of performing surgery on the wrong part of a patient's body. Another report estimates that the average patient in an Intensive Care Unit experiences 1.7 errors per day, one-third of which are potentially life threatening. An estimated 7000 people die annually from medication errors. Hospital patients in the U.S. experience at least, on average, one medication mistake every day. In one year, more than 7 out of every 1000 patients acquired an infection while in a hospital and more than 15 percent of these died. As many as 90,000 Americans die each year from infections they contract while in the hospital.

The problem is not unique to the US. Reportedly, 14,000 deaths or serious injuries occur in Irish hospitals every year as a result of preventable medical errors. The number of adverse events in the hospitals of South Australia is reported to have "soared." In Quebec, annual deaths from preventable medical errors are more than twice the number from road accidents. In all of Canada, preventable medical errors contributed to more than 24,000 deaths in one year.

And the problem, again based on a range of reports, is not getting much better very fast. Six years after the IOM study mentioned above, the same organization indicates there has been little progress in reducing the epidemic of preventable errors. Wrong site surgeries were recently reported to be on the rise, with an increasing number of healthcare facilities having reported mistakenly removing the wrong limb or organ, cutting into the wrong side of bodies, and performing surgery on the wrong patients. I recently read a compelling and well written book with numerous examples of medical errors. The book, Medicine On Trial, describes many of the errors that unfortunately but frequently grace the headlines of today's newspapers and magazines. It speaks of the high numbers of unnecessary patient deaths. The book was written eighteen years ago!

An objective realist believes that where there is smoke there is fire. These statistics and reports are not smoke. They are not fire. They are an inferno, with the blazing flames of human error and wrong behavior that beg for the extinguishing effect of candid observation and follow-through.

Nuclear plant performance is not perfect, and it is not my goal here to pitch nuclear power (although I believe it is a viable energy source for the future). I am impressed with the performance of the nuclear industry and proud of my part in helping it to achieve that performance. By most measures the performance of nuclear plants has improved markedly since the infamous accident at the Three Mile Island nuclear plant. Today, there is a strong focus at the plants on human error reduction. Nuclear operators have ingrained in them practices such as self check and peer check to reduce the likelihood of errors. Errors and near misses are reported, shared with others in the industry and acted on to preclude recurrence. The number of significant events at nuclear plants has decreased by a factor of 60 since the initiation of their safety improvement effort following the Three Mile Island accident. However, the factor that has contributed most to this impressive record is observation. People in the nuclear industry observe performance and then act on those observations to improve performance with a primary focus on safety. Observation is a key element of the improvement effort that has moved nuclear plants from the performance levels of the Three Mile Island era to safety and production levels that are as many as ten times higher today. Do they observe well enough? In many cases, no. This in part was my motivation for starting this book. The basis for my opinion I will discuss in upcoming chapters. But as I observed other industries, and particularly the healthcare industry, I have found that no other industry in the world applies the art of observation to the degree, both in quality and quantity, that the nuclear power industry does. It is to a large degree the success of these nuclear plants upon which much of the following advice is based, offered in the form of concepts and techniques.

Beyond the concepts and techniques that support effective observation, I also provide herein numerous real-life examples to bring additional clarity to those concepts and techniques. I have, as well, defined some terms differently than the reader may understand these terms to mean. This hopefully will provoke thought on fundamental principles that can be applied to a wide range of situations.

To ensure good communication of the concepts and techniques I describe, let me first define what I mean by assessment or observing or watching. (I use these terms interchangeably because I have found that the only assessment worth doing is observation-based.)   Assessment is what managers are doing if they know what's going on in their organizations. It is what managers do, or should be doing, on a daily basis. A manager sitting in a meeting is assessing / observing. She's assessing the people reporting information; the information itself; the people reacting to the information. Walking around an organization is assessing / observing. The walker, if she's doing her job, is assessing -- the people; the conditions. Reviewing a report is also observing --observing the value of the information; the clarity of it; the accuracy of it. Talking to the workforce is observing -- employee morale; attitudes; effectiveness of the communication chain down through the organization. Assessing or observing is part of the daily professional life of managers. They give directions; observe to see what happened as a result of what they told people to do; then give further direction. In fairness to managers, they often do assess or observe -- just not as well as they could.

To simplify terms for the rest of this discussion, I will first lump all of those activities that are not performed as well as they can be, and all of those conditions that are not as good as they can be into one category. They are "problems." They are not "opportunities for improvement"; they are not "issues"; they are not "things that can be done better." They will not, within this book, be described by any of these or other euphemisms which, although they may be kinder to the receiver of the news, give a subtle impression that they really need not be addressed. They are <u>problems</u>! Recognize that if you as a manager find something that you think of and react to as an "opportunity for improvement," you have a problem and you are likely part of it. By not recognizing this newly discovered "opportunity" for what it really is, and that is a "problem"-- and a problem is something that needs correction-- you are unawaredly establishing an expectation that it can remain uncorrected. The subconscious reasoning goes: if the problem is fixed, that is great; but if it is not, that is OK too, because it would just be an "opportunity" missed.

PERFORMANCE-BASED ASSESSMENT

It is important to understand that for assessment to be effective, that is, effective in identifying problems in an organization (or obstacles on the road) that prevent it from achieving its best performance, differentiation needs to be made between assessments performed for compliance, referring to compliance with laws and regulations, and "performance-based" assessments. A performance-based assessment identifies <u>any</u> problem that affects performance, regardless of whether or not it is in compliance with regulations, laws, or other requirements. There are no specific criteria for defining these problems. Rather they must be recognized as such by the observer drawing on his experience and the experience of others. The only litmus test for a performance-based problem is that when such a problem is corrected, the performance of the organization improves. Unfortunately such is not the case for every compliance problem that is corrected.

Consider the contrast between performance-based assessments and compliance-based assessments, the latter often being called audits. Audits of compliance verify that applicable requirements are met. These audits are good. Among other of their benefits, they keep us out of jail. But they're not good enough. Unfortunately, as you watch the news and listen to most of the business talk these days, you will find that most assessment activities are of the compliance-oriented, not-good-enough type. There is a reason for this that I'll touch on shortly, but first the contrast.

A compliance audit verifies that the rules or laws are adhered to. But rules don't cover every case. They can't. For example, a rule may require that a certain number of workers need to be present in some particular operating facility during some particular activity or time. That is an easily definable requirement. For discussion purposes, let's say that number is twelve. The compliance-based overseer (or observer) walks into the facility, counts the number of workers, finds twelve, and leaves satisfied. But what if one of the workers also has other responsibilities? Does that mean the worker is only partially there since he is only partially dedicated to the work in question? What if one of the workers has another job that has kept him awake all night and consequently is considerably less attentive in his sleep-deprived stupor? Should he be counted as one of the twelve? The examples could go on and on. For each example, the rules can be rewritten to cover that specific problem. But as this happens, the rules become more and more numerous and complex and more and more constraining on the organization. In reality, this often happens. That's why we have such a complex legal system in the United States. National Review magazine, in an October

1995 issue, pointed out that (as a comparative measure), The "Lord's Prayer" is 66 words; the "Gettysburg Address" is 286 words; there are 1,322 words in the "Declaration of Independence". In contrast, the article went on to say that government regulations on the sale of cabbage total 26,911 words! On regulation of Cabbage!

This tendency to write more and more rules is why many organizations have volumes upon volumes of policies and procedures on their shelves. These tomes are often unread and not understood, in large part because of their volume. If you have these large volumes of policy in your organization, examine your conscience. Every time there's a problem, do you write a new rule? Every time a rule is broken, do you rewrite the rule? During my time on nuclear submarines, the entire set of policies governing the operation and maintenance of these very complex nuclear machines, was referred to as "the blue book." It was about a quarter inch thick and contained all the policy that was needed. But its content was all substance. There were no superfluous policies, and the content rarely changed. On those unusual occasions when a policy was violated, the violator got fixed, not the policy. The system worked well, and the adherence to these policies was a key contributor to the U.S. nuclear navy having the safest nuclear operating history in the world. This is the kind of result that comes from performance-based thinking. It is also demonstrative of a concept I will describe later that can be used to achieve more consistent adherence to policies.

In summary, "performance-based" is a term you should not forget, and one that you will find useful in guiding your observation activities. If you are the manager of your home, remember it. If you are a business manager, write it down. Put it on a sign and hang it over your desk to remind those reporting to you that this is what you want, indeed, what you need.

1. *THINK PERFORMANCE-BASED*

This is AACT 1, the first of many Applied Assessment Concepts and Techniques (AACTs) that are shared in this book. They are the heart of the guidance that I have found to be most useful in training and coaching both the experienced and the inexperienced in the field of observation. These AACTs are compiled in an easily referenced index at the end of this book. They can be applied to managing as well as observing. This symmetry of the AACTs across a plane between management and observation is not coincidental, for a good manager is a good observer and a good observer is looking for the effects of good management.

Hopefully, for the reader, the AACTs will help with both -- as you apply an observant eye.

CHAPTER 2
THE ENABLING FOUNDATION
FOR SEEING
THE GOOD, THE BAD, AND
THE UGLY

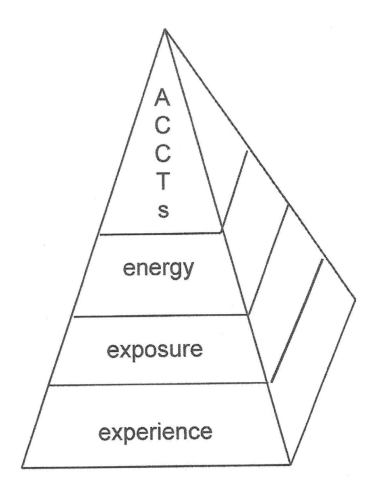

Fig 1. Requisite Attributes of a Good Observer

The list of attributes that one would "like" for an observer to have is considerably longer than the list of those that are vital to his success. An argument can be made that a person has to be well spoken, so he can clearly articulate problems he uncovers; that he needs strong interpersonal skills, so he will maintain effective working relationships with those being observed; that he has to have problem analysis skills, which allow him to analyze problems in greater detail; and the list could go on. But those are more the frosting on the cake of attributes rather than essential ingredients of the cake itself.

2. EXPERIENCE, EXPOSURE, AND ENERGY ARE THE REQUISITE ATTRIBUTES OF A GOOD OBSERVER

As depicted in figure 1, these attributes are the foundation upon which any advancement in observation skill, including that achieved through use of the AACTs described in this book, must be based. Without these requisite attributes the observer won't have to worry about analyzing problems since it's likely he won't identify them. He won't be able to see the good, the bad, and the ugly, or to recognize them if he does see them.

This, the second of the AACTs presented here, forms the underpinning of a sound observation effort -- a capable person. Given a choice, select the person who has even traces of these attributes over the person who has the strongest of ancillary traits yet lacks one of these vital elements of experience, exposure, and energy. Keep in mind that, as stated earlier, a person may have a primary job as an observer or assessor, but observing is also a vital part of any manager's job. Consequently, these three elements are vital to the success of any manager. Internalization of the concepts and techniques described in this book puts a fine point on the total characteristics package of a good observer, but that point must rest on the foundation of experience, exposure, and energy.

Experience

The most important of these vital attributes is experience, that is, experience in the activities being observed. These activities encompass more than those technical aspects unique to any particular field. In fact, it is the non-technical aspects of activities that are typically involved when human errors occur, and thus are the ones most important to observe. This has been shown time and again in the analysis of errors in the nuclear as well as the healthcare industry, but it also makes sense intuitively. In professions that require highly complex work, or where the consequences of an improperly performed activity are significant, the players are typically well trained in the technical areas and are required to have considerable experience and education before being left to perform on their own. Consequently, the technical aspects of their work can reasonably be expected to be performed well. However, the same high level of training and experience that leads to technical expertise also breeds complacency regarding more routine matters, such as ensuring one is about to operate the right component in a nuclear plant (or operate on the right patient in a hospital). It is, therefore, important not only that the observer have experience, but that she have broad enough experience to effectively observe these non – technical aspects. This experience may well come from technical fields different from the one being observed. For example, an airline pilot who has never seen a nuclear plant can provide valuable constructive feedback after observing the staff in a nuclear plant control room -- because the pilot has related experience. She has experience in the interaction of personnel as they manage potentially hazardous activities. The pilot is not observing the control of reactivity in the reactor. She is observing the interaction and teamwork of the control room crew, an attribute vital to the crew's success. Likewise, a nuclear engineer can provide valuable feedback after observing surgery in a hospital operating room -- because the engineer has related experience. He has experience in activities that require exceptional attention to detail. The engineer is not observing surgical techniques. He is observing the control of medical instruments and supplies with eyes experienced in observing control methods that are designed to prevent foreign material from being inadvertently left in nuclear components (not unlike leaving a gauze pad or a needle inside of a patient).

This type of broad experience is essential. If an observer lacks it, she needs to either get it or get a different job. Many nuclear companies feel so strongly about the importance of observers having experience that not only is it a prerequisite for hiring, it is also required that the experience be maintained relatively fresh. The freshness is achieved by either having the observers periodically fill the role of line managers, or by periodically rotating line managers into observer positions. To unleash an inexperienced observer on an organization, is asking for trouble. Problems will be found by the inexperienced observer. Some of these findings may even be valuable. But over time, the inexperienced will resort to the only tools they have -- theories, or what others have written in books (and sometimes never really practiced themselves). Not only will little value be added to the organization, but also, at one time or another, actions will be required to be taken by line management, in response to baseless findings that will not only add little value, but worse yet, will deflect management attention by competing with truly valid priorities.

Exposure

The second vital attribute is exposure -- exposure to what "good" looks like in the activities being observed. A person has to know what good looks like or she or he will never be able to recognize when it is or isn't there. Likewise, what one has seen as "good" is the measuring stick by which one differentiates between the bad and the ugly, and is therefore able to communicate this perspective on the problem. Again, exposure is a vital trait. If an observer doesn't have it, he needs to get it. It isn't hard to get, but it does take effort. It requires getting out and seeing how other people do things. Priority needs to be placed on getting to those places widely recognized as being "good." But to know what good is in the many areas that an observer should be looking at requires <u>frequently</u> getting out to see how others do things, whenever the opportunity presents itself. People who are good at anything in the long term are that way because they continuously look for ways to improve what they do and how they do it. Consequently, "good" is ever changing, and benchmarks move ever higher. Also, in some organizations, good comes and then it goes -- because of complacency, loss of strong leadership, or other factors. And finally, remember that "good" is relative. Anything better than what you do is "good."

Consider the following example in light of the statistic that each year more than 7000 deaths result from medication errors that take place both in and out of hospitals. The example actually happened to a close relative of mine who was receiving medical treatment in his home because of his age and medical condition. Think of how you, as a layperson, would react if this happened to one of your family members -- to your Mother for example. Your Mother is receiving a blood thinning medication (Coumadin). In thinning the blood, Coumadin reduces the potential for death or serious harm that might come from blood clotting where and when it shouldn't, such as in a blood vessel supplying blood flow to the brain or heart. The accuracy of the Coumadin dose provided to any patient is particularly important. Too little of the medication and the blood thickens to the point of allowing a fatal blockage as just mentioned. Too much and the blood thins to a point where the protective mechanism of blood clotting is not available. If, while a patient's blood is in this highly thinned state, a serious cut, or worse yet, undetectable internal bleeding occurs, the patient may even die. In this example, internal bleeding is likely to occur because of a number of other ailments characteristic of your Mother's advanced age. To guard against this, the blood of the patient is frequently tested to ensure the Coumadin dose is maintained correctly for the current condition of the blood. Because of a series of errors, that you will only hear about later, your Mother at one point receives a dose of Coumadin that is almost twice that prescribed by her doctor. You then learn that, almost unbelievably, she received this over-dosage again and again, over a period of a week. As a result, her blood is thinned to the point of substantially increasing the risk to her health and possibly even to her life. Fortunately, because your Mother eventually recalls the amount of Coumadin she should be taking, the problem gets identified and corrected before serious harm or death can result. You then learn that the problem began when the dose of Coumadin that was provided was drawn from a medication container that was clearly labeled with a dose that was higher than what should have been administered at the time. This dose had been correct at the time the medication bottle was labeled, but was based on an analysis of your Mother's blood, and both the blood analysis and the container labeling had been done a week earlier. Since that time, based on more recent blood analyses that indicate your Mother's blood was thin enough, the doctor ordered a lower dose of the medication. The lower dose had been communicated by the doctor to a caregiver, over the phone. This information was then not passed on to a second caregiver who would be the one to administer your Mother's daily medications. When time came for the medication, the uninformed caregiver assumed the medication dose had not changed, found the medication container with the clearly labeled but unfortunately out-of-date dose, and provided it to your Mother as directed on the label -- again and again, over a week's time. After the error was identified and corrective action had been taken, you have a discussion with the caregivers involved and are told in a somewhat dismissive way, "It was only a communication problem," and "No harm was done." Little concern is expressed over the increased risk and the potential for harm to have occurred. Other than relying on a single person to ensure future doses are correct, little else is done to preclude recurrence of the problem.

You intuitively know that something must be wrong with a system that would allow your Mother, in an environment of care, to be given something that would harm her. The fact that the incorrect dose was that of Coumadin and not some more powerful medication that could have led to even greater potential for harm, and faster, was a function of fate, rather than of any preventive measures purposely put in place. But without exposure to some of the best methods of controlling medication, all you can ask are general questions such as, "How did this happen?" On the other hand, if you have had the EXPOSURE to what much better medication controls look like, you can ask more probing questions such as, how was the telephone message from the doctor verified to have been heard correctly. Was the Doctor's order written down? Why not? How was the information transferred between caregivers? Was this verified to have been done accurately? Contrast what happened in the above example with what happens during the administration of medication in a hospital when it is necessary for a doctor to prescribe a medication over the telephone:

1.   The doctor tells the caregiver what drug to administer, the dose, and the frequency. Upon hearing the order, the caregiver writes this information on a physician's order form. (This eliminates the possibility of the receiver hearing the correct informa-

tion but then, because of a distraction, later recalling it incorrectly. This practice constitutes the first barrier against a medication error.)

2. After writing the information on the physician order form, the caregiver reads the information back to the physician to ensure that the information has been correctly received and understood. (This practice of "read-back" has been implemented in many healthcare facilities because of the high incidence of medication errors, and constitutes the second barrier to error.)

3. The medication information is transferred from the physician's order form to a formal Medication Administration Record (MAR). The MAR is a document that is specific to the patient and serves as a record of each medication the patient is to receive, the amount, and the frequency with which it is to be administered. The information transcribed to the MAR is then checked by a second person to ensure it has been correctly transcribed from the written physician's order. (Barrier number three.)

4. The caregiver who is to administer the medication takes the MAR to the patient's bedside, verifies the identity of the patient with that shown on the MAR, checks the name and dosage of medication as written in the MAR against that which is about to be administered to the patient, and if correct, administers it. (Barrier number four.)

Given that the administration of medication is so much better controlled in a hospital than it is in when the patient is in home care, another valid question to be asked is, Why? Why were none of the four barriers or anything similar to them in place to protect your Mother? These are questions an effective observer could ask. In the response to them would be a picture of the performance of those responsible for, as well as those directly involved in, administering the medication. Without having been exposed to the better controls, these questions would likely not be asked.

Each of the above barriers that could have been in place but were not is a problem. A common shortfall of weaker observers is not recognizing a problem when they see it (such as lack of a barrier used by others). Some confuse this inability to recognize problems with a lack of high standards, thinking the observer sees and recognizes the problem situation or condition, but believes it to be OK and is therefore willing to accept it. Such may be the case, but more likely the person sees but does not recognize the condition or activity as a problem, because she hasn't seen how much better that condition or activity can be, as shown by other organizations.

Energy

The third vital attribute is energy. What does high energy look like? It looks like a person who moves quickly; covers a lot of ground; never sees an unsolvable problem; volunteers for more even when he has a full plate of work; goes well out of his way to examine every aspect of a problem; starts early, works late; swaps his suit for work clothes and gets out in the trenches with the workforce to see where the problems really are. A high energy observer is continuously pulling strings (a technique for follow-up that will be discussed later). When he doggedly follows a lead and pulls on a string for hours of his otherwise free time, and the lead eventually takes him to a dead end, which occasionally happens, what does he do? He immediately grabs another string and starts pulling. He does not spend time complaining or lamenting. High energy applied to follow-up and the resultant ability to develop the most valuable insight during observations is the primary reason that the best of observers stand out among their peers.

The following is a practical example of what high energy looks like: I recently conducted an observation at a facility that had to be completed in two days. I arrived late on a Monday night, and had to have my report ready for verbal delivery before noon on the following Thursday. Prior to arriving at the facility, I spent twenty-nine hours preparing. This included reviewing over eight hundred and fifty documents. While at the facility, I spent thirty-five hours inside the working spaces and interviewed twenty two people. At noon on Thursday I delivered a four page report that included reinforcement of six positive points I had observed and eleven problem areas along with the bases for concluding these were problems.

How does one get high energy? You can't. You either have it or you don't. I tried for years to coach various people on how to improve their energy level. I lead by example and preached until hoarse on what high energy looks like and what kind of behaviors should be practiced and exhibited. I failed in every case. I now believe that a person's energy level comes about through a complex combination of life experiences over years; work ethic of families; early job experiences; and other unknown factors, all of which solidify into an unchangeable form by the time a person enters the workforce, possibly even before then. Energy level can be "tweaked" but not significantly changed. However, high energy is easy to identify, just by watching someone work. Factor it into your selection process and never hire anyone who doesn't demonstrate high energy -- for any job, and least of all for a job that involves observing.

A NOTE OF CAUTION

Beware of the assessor who is "surprised" when a problem that he has failed to find reveals itself, and then, in an attempt to justify why he had not identified it, blames any of a myriad of external factors, none of which are under his control. He might blame a lack of clarity in the assessment process; or fault the training provided or not provided by someone else; or allege an overload of work that he claims precludes the thoroughness of his assessments. Don't buy it. Years of experience in the assessment field have shown me time and again that shortfalls in performance related to things happening, about which people who should have been aware were not, in addition to being the fault of the responsible line manager, are also clearly the fault of the assessor. That fault, in the majority of cases, will be linked to a weakness in one or more of the three fundamental attributes listed above, none of which an underperforming assessor will likely either recognize or be willing to admit.

CHAPTER 3
SOME FUNDAMENTAL AaCTs

Given that the observer has the basic building blocks in the enabling foundation of her make-up, as described in chapter two, the fine point on the pyramid of observer capability is the application of concepts and techniques (or AaCTs).

The strength and stability of a pyramid come from the inherent strength of its triangular surfaces. The strength of each triangular surface in turn is derived from the fact that its shape is defined totally by angles that cannot change. Each of the angles is determined by the length of its opposing side. Since the length of the side cannot change, the angle is similarly unchangeable and stability results. Thus, without the point or vertex (or AaCTs), the observer's assemblage of abilities will never achieve the full strength, stability, and effectiveness of a complete pyramid. As the complete pyramid is differentiated from the truncated version by its strength, the use of these applied assessment concepts and techniques, or AaCTs, similarly differentiates the best of the observers from the rest. It is these AaCTs to which this book is dedicated.

This chapter deals with some of those fundamental AACTs that, along with the two already mentioned, are applicable in all observation settings. The first of these AACTs is to recognize that,

3. *THERE ARE ALWAYS PROBLEMS OUT THERE*

Your job is to find them. This is a matter of mindset, and it need not be a negative mindset. Dr. Norman Vincent Peale said it well when he said, essentially, every problem has in it the seed of its own solution. If you have no problems, you have no seeds. If you have convinced yourself that performance is fine, then that is what you'll see when you observe performance. Our minds tend to justify conclusions we have already drawn. If on the other hand, one accepts reality, and reality is that there is always something out there that can be done better (a "problem" as referred to here) then one's eyes and ears will be tuned to find those things. This concept can be applied in any environment, whether it's reviewing a document, walking around an office, a hospital, a production facility, or talking to people, either in an interview or in casual conversation.

As a simple exercise to further emphasize the above point, take a piece of paper and write down a description of the room in which you are currently sitting. Limit this to a couple of minutes so as to first not waste your time and second, to force you to capture the most descriptive elements of the room.

Now put that paper aside. Take another piece of paper and, being as critical as you can, write down everything in the room that is a "problem," that is, everything that you would change if you were in a high stakes contest competing to make the room the most perfect setting (for whatever purpose the room was initially designed.)

Now compare what is written on the two pieces of paper. It is most likely that the first description you wrote will contain none of the items that are in the second, more critical description. Why? The answer is because it is not natural (for other than the trained observer) to look for things that are wrong. But if your goal is to truly make this the best room in the world, which description will provide more value?

Don't discount the little exercise above as trivial. A number of facilities with exemplary conditions in their work areas achieved that level in part by designating "model areas," where the cleanliness, storage, lighting, equipment marking, and painting were moved to the highest level that could be achieved. These spaces were then used as a model to show the workforce what was expected of them in terms of maintaining their work spaces.

INDUSTRIAL TOURISM

A corollary to the above principle is, when you are looking at any facility or organization,

4. DON'T BE AN INDUSTRIAL TOURIST

"Industrial tourism" is what occurs in most facilities when an observer who lacks a critical eye walks around the place and just gawks at the things around him. This is not unlike a tourist in the big city who stares at the tall buildings, looking for nothing in particular, and at the end of the day, can say nothing more profound than, "Wow! Big place! Tall buildings! Lots of people!" The critical observer knows there is something out there that is a problem and is driven to find it. She looks intently. She goes out of her way to crawl into the remote corners of a place. She exerts the extra effort to link up with workers, asking them questions about their work, the state of the company, new management initiatives. She continually asks herself questions such as these: Why is that item where it is? Why is there dirt in that corner? Why is portable equipment stored in the hallway? How might a cluttered hallway inhibit egress in the event of a fire? Why are there not more people around when this is within the normal working hours? Or conversely, if the case, why are there so many people around and so few that seem to be doing anything? These questions never end.

Now if you accept that problems are out there, and if you agree that walking around like an industrial tourist is what you should <u>not</u> do, then what is it that you <u>should</u> do? The answer is, look for specific problems, because,

5. *YOU WON'T FIND WHAT YOU AREN'T LOOKING FOR*

Give some thought to the following questions: How clean was the area around where you last parked your car? How short and clean were the fingernails of the last food handler you dealt with? How clear and understandable was the labeling of produce in the last grocery store where you shopped? For how many seconds did the nurse at the doctor's office wash his hands before treating you? (Healthcare guidelines indicate that a minimum of 15 seconds of vigorously rubbing all parts of the hands together is the minimum required to ensure the elimination of harmful infection-spreading bacteria.) It's likely you wouldn't be able to answer these questions. However, if you were properly motivated, that is, if someone said they would pay you a thousand dollars for each correct answer to the above questions, and you could go back and revisit those activities, there is no doubt you would easily be able to identify information you missed on the first go around. Why? The answer is because on the first round you were an industrial tourist. On the second round, you were an observer, motivated to find things that need fixing, and carrying a list, mental or otherwise, of things to look for. More about this when we get to AACT 17 [USE 3X5 CARDS]

THE UNSEEN PROBLEM

6. PROBLEMS COME IN EITHER OF TWO FORMS -- THINGS THAT ARE DONE INCORRECTLY, AND THINGS THAT ARE NOT DONE BUT SHOULD BE. THE LATTER ARE FREQUENTLY OVERLOOKED

Many observers overlook important problems because they get so caught up in looking for deficiencies in the conditions, processes, or activities they are seeing, that they forget to look for conditions, processes, and activities they are not seeing. It is a simple but worthwhile exercise, after reviewing with a critical eye all aspects of an operation, to ask yourself, in addition to whatever problems you have seen, what problems have you <u>not</u> seen that exist because of the <u>absence</u> of some condition, process, or activity. For example, one could observe the operating and maintenance activities on any piece of complex technical equipment and conclude, upon seeing no deficiencies, that all is well. However, a more accurate conclusion would be that all is well with what has been observed. But what about what has not been observed? There may very well be a problem with the equipment that has not yet manifested itself. I once worked at a facility that had several hundred large valves designed to open automatically and relieve pressure in various components when internal pressures reached specified values. The valves had been physically inspected numerous times and always looked good. Maintenance activities such as periodic lubrication were also observed. Again these were performed well. The problem was that these valves were "passive" components that normally just sat there and did nothing. They were only required to operate in extreme and rare circumstances. As luck would have it, these circumstances had not occurred for years. Unfortunately, neither had any of the valves ever been tested since installation, over ten years earlier. When tested, most of the valves were found to be defective. They would not have operated properly had the conditions requiring their operation ever arisen -- a deficiency that would only have been identified had someone, in the absence of observed deficiencies, asked the question, what have we <u>not</u> observed?

WHAT IS "WRONG"?

An important question that needs to be considered before pursuing the art of observation is: What makes something "wrong"? Similar to the point made in the discussion of "problems" earlier, if you're interested in excellent performance,

7. *WRONG IS ANYTHING THAT ISN'T AS GOOD AS IT CAN BE*

Obviously this is not to say that every deficiency in the universe of assessment is as important as every other one. More will be said about this and the fine art of prioritization later. However, a good observer never overlooks what at first glance may be a minor deficiency or even something unusual. The significance of some seemingly minor defect may turn out to be a lot more significant when viewed in the light of other information. While observing activities in one unit of a hospital, I once was struck by the similarities between all of the entries on a check-off sheet on which someone had indicated by their initials that they had verified the presence of all necessary backup surgical supplies in a locker. Each entry had been made with the same color ink, apparently by the same person, with the same writing style. The written initials seemed to be equally aged. Suspecting (but being unable to prove) that all of the entries were made at the same time thereby hiding the fact that the supply checks were routinely not being done, I made note of the item. It wasn't until two days and multiple observations later when it became evident that ready availability of supplies, such as rubber gloves and bandages, was frequently a problem. A number of incidents had already occurred as a result of not having backup supplies readily available when they were needed. Only at this time, did the significance of my earlier observation become apparent and also become a useful piece of information in putting together a compelling story to hospital executives that action was needed to ensure the backup supplies were regularly and properly verified to be available.

You might ask, How do you know what is not "as good as it can be"? Review AACT 2 [EXPERIENCE, EXPOSURE, AND ENERGY ARE THE REQUISITE ATTRIBUTES OF A GOOD OBSERVER.] The answer to the question lies in the element of "exposure." Compare everything you look at with the best you have ever seen -- be it a place, a condition, or even an attitude. Regarding the example just discussed, organizations often use routine check-off lists to ensure ready availability of important equipment. In some facilities, these are sloppily maintained; in some cases not routinely checked and initialed, but rather initialed after the fact, sometimes after many hours have passed. I once visited a healthcare facility at which the record sheet indicating hourly turning of patients to prevent bed sores were routinely only initialed as having been done at the end of every 12 hour period. The manager responsible for the area in which these checks were performed was aware of and unbothered by this. He saw the initials as only a requirement of policy. As long as the patient turnings were done (as he <u>trusted</u> they had been) and all of the appropriate spaces were initialed before his shift left the facility, he saw no problem with the practice as it was performed. (This manager was on the losing side of the argument because of the concept of performance-based assessment. The same week in which this discussion took place, a patient developed a significant pressure ulcer or bed sore because a nurse had forgotten to do one or more of the routine turnings and no one else had caught the lapse.) At the other and more positive end of the quality spectrum lie those facilities wherein routine checks are meticulously performed and initialed, with an expectation that anyone walking by such check lists would look at them to ensure the latest check had been performed. At some facilities, an additional set of initials is required to indicate supervisory assurance of proper performance and documentation of the checks. Those that are sloppily maintained are "wrong" -- because they are not as good as they can be. In such cases, at least make a note of the observation and plan on further analyzing the collected information and sorting out its relative significance later.

One caution regarding finding things that are "wrong" is,

8. *DIFFERENT IS NOT WRONG*

Just because someone chooses to do something differently from how you or some other observer does or would do it, doesn't make it wrong. This shortfall of calling everything that is different wrong, is commonly exhibited by peers involved in but inexperienced in observation activities. Once directly stated, the point seems obvious. However, reinforcing it before the start of an assessment sensitizes those that might otherwise fall into the time-wasting trap of collecting and analyzing information on a non-problem. A good acid test to use in determining whether some thing is wrong or simply different is to ask,

9. *SO WHAT?*

Ask this question of any statement of an alleged problem. This in some ways is an application of AACT 1

[THINK PERFORMANCE BASED]. If there is not a clear and compelling answer to this question, forget the item. Don't waste your time pursuing it any further. Move on to something that has a consequence, something the correction of which will improve the performance of the organization. If there is a clear and compelling answer to the question, then make sure that answer is included in any description of the problem. Otherwise, someone informed of the problem may not be polite enough to spend time pondering what the consequences of the issue might be, and may disregard it out of hand.

BEING SELF-CRITICAL

I once spent a few days at an organization whose performance had slipped over several years and continued to slip even as I visited the place. They went from being a widely recognized top performer that many others wanted to emulate, to one that was at best mediocre and still sliding on its way down. After pointing out a number of what I considered deficient practices and conditions at the facility to several of my hosts, who easily recognized the issues once pointed out, the hosts said, "I guess we need to be more self-critical." Beyond being a remarkable understatement, their response revealed that they would be well advised to emulate some of the more successful organizations, which have in one way or another established an internal expectation to,

10. *LET NO ONE BE MORE CRITICAL OF YOU THAN YOU*

Whenever someone from outside an organization identifies a shortfall or deficiency in that organization, the leadership of that organization should get answers to the following questions: 1. Is the point valid? And 2. If it is valid, why didn't we identify it? The viewpoint here needs to be, if there is a valid obstacle on the road to improved performance, why weren't the drivers (or the lookouts) of the organization able to see it? The answer to this question and the subsequent corrective action that precludes its recurrence are crucial to continuing improvement. More importantly from the perspective of the observer, the answer to the above questions and whether or not AACT 10 is imbued in the organization are important pieces of the picture puzzle that, when assembled, will depict the effectiveness of that organization.

Even when one recognizes the importance of being self-critical, it is hard to be critical of something that you have given birth to, either figuratively or literally. When you design a process, or develop a program, or perform or direct an activity, the natural tendency is to think whatever you have done is great, or at a minimum, good. It's beautiful. It's like your child, your baby. This is natural, but counterproductive to improving. If you want to make whatever you have done better,

11. *YOU HAVE TO BE WILLING TO CALL YOUR BABY UGLY*

Terms similar to this have been applied to various business principles, but rarely if ever to the field of assessment. You may find these words shocking. It is something almost taboo, to call any baby, let alone your own, ugly. Such a reaction gives credibility to the value of understanding the concept. Few would come to the conclusion on their own that there is value in calling their baby ugly. It would be unnatural. But actively identifying problems in your babies (the activities or areas you own) and describing them candidly to capture how ugly they really are, is the first step in correcting them. An effective observer will keep this concept in mind and use it to interpret spoken words and understand motivation when interacting with the birth mother of any program or process being reviewed.

GRAY INFORMATION

An important differentiating characteristic that separates the good observers from the mediocre is the ability to deal with the almost infinite amount of information related to any subject. This information lies on a spectrum that is almost infinitely long in both the positive and the negative directions. The information of value in observations, however, is only that which lies in a relatively small percentage on each far end. One end is valuable negative information, which for simplicity we'll call "black"; the other is valuable positive information, which we'll call "white." Everything else is "gray" information. The applicable technique here is,

12. *IGNORE THE GRAY INFORMATION*

Gray information will only unnecessarily tax your information processing capability. It is the kind of information that provides no value in distinguishing the quality of an activity, place, or document from any other in the universe. It therefore provides no value in judging the quality or effectiveness of a subject being examined. For example, it would likely take several pages to describe the activity of a nurse administering medication to a patient. This would include the facts that,

- The nurse read the physician's order for the medication.
- The medication was requested from the pharmacy.
- The pharmacy backed up the physician by checking to ensure the medication would not adversely interact with any other medication the patient was taking.
- The pharmacy delivered the medication to the nursing station.
- The nurse transported the medication to the patient's bedside.

- The patient took the medication after being handed the pill-form medication along with a glass of water.
- The nurse returned to the patient at a later time to ensure the medication had the desired effect.
- And more ....

However, all of this is gray information. It describes the same activities that go on thousands of times each day in most hospitals. There may, however, be an instance when a patient is given the wrong dose of medication, or perhaps an inaccurate dose -- for example, by administering a hoped-for 250 milligram dose by breaking a 500 milligram tablet in half even though the tablet was not scored to ensure even breaking. This would be black information. Similarly, the nurse may have requested a co-worker to verify the medication provided was in fact the correct one in the correct amount. Such unrequired but conscientious (and unusual) behavior to reduce the likelihood of error would be white information. Both of the latter two statements convey information that differentiates the latter examples of medication administration from the uncountable numbers of satisfactorily conducted medication administrations that occur routinely. Because they allow one to differentiate and evaluate this activity, each of these statements, therefore, is of value in assessment, and, therefore, is valuable to the observer.

Collecting gray information, on the other hand, expends time and energy, with no payback. Application of this concept is just as important, and often even more important, for the watched as it is for the watcher. It is not in the best interest of the observed for the observer to collect gray information. The nurse that would be observed in the example above has better things to do than describe every detail of the medication administration procedure to an observer when that observer could just as well read it on his own time. Collecting gray information is generally a valueless activity. Avoid it.

A good observer knows how to quickly get to the valuable edges of the information spectrum, particularly in areas where there is a generally recognized need for improvement. The following is an example of how this concept can be applied: In an oversight organization, the myriad of procedures that describe how an organization does business, its routine activities, and the makeup of the group, are informational elements that fall in the gray zone. Conversely, the kind of evaluative information that lies at the outer edges of the information spectrum and that can be used to quickly assess the effectiveness of the function comes from questions that push into the black or white zones, such as "Does the oversight organization find problems before they become self-revealing or before they're found by outside organizations?" If the answer to this bottom-line-type question is yes, then the organization is doing its job, at least in this one respect, and the rest of that gray information doesn't matter. If the answer to the question is no, then a problem has been identified, and the next step is to understand why that problem is occurring. Again, information dealing with the cause of the problem can also be considered to lie on a black to white spectrum of information, and should be processed in the same way.

PLANS AND THEIR VALUE

Here's another concept worth keeping in mind:

"The best laid schemes o' mice an' men gang aft a gley."

The importance of communicating in clear and widely understood terms will be discussed later. For now, accept the importance of clear communication; recognize the above statement may not be clear; and consider the version restated in more modern English:

"The best laid plans of mice and men often go awry."

This is a jewel of knowledge applicable to observations but not likely recognized as such by its author, the Scottish poet Robert Burns, when he wrote this in his poem, "To a Mouse."

This adage makes it evident that even as far back as the 1700's some people recognized that plans by themselves aren't worth a Tinker's dam (given that Tinkers, or those who repair pots and pans, no longer have need for the dams they once used.) It's the implementation of plans that produce results. Programs (which can be viewed as synonymous with plans) are no more than intentions to do things. Similarly, considering that plans carry with them no guarantee of action, the tool to keep in mind in any discussion of problem resolution efforts is,

13. *FOCUS ON IMPLEMENTATION*

Provided that a question intended to probe problem resolution efforts has been properly phrased to get to results, as it should be, even mention of the word "program" or "plan" in the response of the person being interviewed should be a red flag. The flag should warn the observer that the person responding likely has no results to speak of, and is masking this lack of results by discussing programs or plans -- that she hopes will lead to results.

The inability to articulate results because of their absence is most likely to be true when a program or plan has only recently been implemented. Take any odds that if a program is new and the responsible manager has not made a conscientious and specific effort to observe and track results, and to ensure the program is working, that it is not. The tendency to put programs or other paper fixes in place rather than focus on the actions needed to fix problems is a natural organizational response. It is much more comfortable in addressing a problem to write something down on a piece of paper, such as a program, than it is to change behaviors. The latter usually involves confronting some person and telling that person he or she needs to do a better job. This tendency toward paper fixes is also fostered by the perceived need to prove to officials, regulators, politicians, and often the public, that we have done something tangible -- we have created a program. But, as valuable as they can be, programs or plans are little more than what someone has written on a piece of paper. Problems are not caused by paper or lack of paper; they are caused by people. Consequently, development of a program or plan, by itself, won't fix or preclude problems. Unfortunately this is often the fix targeted by weaker organizations. Recall the evacuation and emergency response plans that were developed in some southern states but untested by implementation until the 2006 hurricane season.

An example of focusing on paper rather than implementation, and one repeated many times in my experience, occurred in an organization that was having a problem with the method of ensuring the safety of maintenance workers. This method involves using temporary tags that are attached to certain valves to ensure personnel are aware that the valves are to remain closed to isolate a work area and thus protect the workers from the scalding hot fluids confined behind the valves. An internal review of the problem, which basically was that these valves were found open when they should not have been, had determined that its root cause was the inadequacy of the valve tagging procedure. I was requested to verify their conclusion. Within several hours, after observing the valves and tags and discussing them with a number of workers and supervisors, I concluded:

- People who installed the tags were required to complete a qualification on the method; however, once qualified, even if the person did not apply one of these tags for years, the person was never required to either re-qualify, refresh her qualifications, or to maintain her proficiency in tag installation.

- Management expectations regarding verification of installed tags were not understood by a wide range of workers. The facility's procedure for tagging these valves clearly stated on which valves the tags were to be independently verified to be properly placed. Yet some workers thought that all tags had to be independently verified, while some thought only tags on valves in certain areas had to be verified. A complicating factor in the problem was that the procedure contained the term "independently verified," and there was a wide range of understanding of what this meant and how it was to be accomplished.

- The tagging procedure had been recently changed, and although the change to the program was not very extensive, the rollout of the change was done poorly. Most people were unaware of what changes had been made to the program, and in some cases, were even unaware that that the program had been changed.

Clearly in the above example, a number of managers had not done their jobs. But going after the procedure rather than the implementation of it was the easier and more comfortable thing to do because it required no confrontation of anyone.

As another example, I once visited a facility where it was internally recognized by senior management that the middle-level managers were not spending enough time in the work place, seeing what the workers were doing and providing coaching. To address this problem, management had recently implemented a program whereby a green card was required to be used by a manager when he went into the field. He was to write down on the card whatever he saw that needed correction, and submit the card to a data bank. Prior to this program, another program, very similar to this one had been launched. The earlier program required both orange cards and white cards to be used in a similar but slightly different manner -- orange cards being used for more significant problems and white cards for less significant ones. This program was still alive, but not doing very well as evident by the inconsequential number of cards that had been submitted in the last year. The facility also had a "Zone Inspection Program" that required each manager to be assigned to a zone in the facility, and to periodically inspect that zone and ensure management expectations were being met. This program was also not in good health. Some signs in the various zones, intended to publicize the identity of the manager responsible for that zone, listed managers who were no longer with the company. Considering all of the programmatic descriptions of these white cards and orange cards, and green cards, and zone inspections to be "gray"" information, I ignored them. After my personal observations clearly indicated managers were still not spending time in the work place, I asked several middle-level managers if their bosses had ever directly and clearly told them how much time they were expected to spend in the workplace and what they were expected to do during that time. The answer was unfortunately, but clearly, no. Additionally they also commented that their bosses spent even less time in the workplace than they did. This latter comment was useful insight into what the real problem was.

The bottom line on this point is that whenever the subject of a "program" comes up in an assessment discussion, the only thing the observer needs to pursue is how well it is working.

INSIGHT

A Chinese statesman, in the early 1700's said that taking action to solve a problem is easy. Gaining understanding, so that one knows what problem to solve, is hard. Understanding a problem comes from having insight into what might be causing it, and that, in turn, comes from, in one form or another, asking WHY? Consequently, another highly valuable technique for an observer is

14. *APPLY Y CUBED*

(Or for those not mathematically inclined, apply "Y? Y? Y?")

This is a shorthand way to remember to continually ask why and to ask this multiple times in succession, in various discussion lines. I have found the number 3 to be a useful guideline. This gets sufficiently into the problem to gain insight on how to correct it, but does not take the discussion to such a high and general level that it no longer yields actionable information. Here's an actual example: A seemingly minor problem noted at one facility was that the floor was dirty. What action would you expect? Sweep the floor?

Applying the principle of Y CUBED provides a different perspective on this simple observation:

The floor is dirty.

Question: **Why** (is the floor dirty)?

Response: Following work that generates a lot of dirt, workers don't clean up after themselves and the janitorial staff only sweeps the floor once a week.

Question: **Why** (don't the workers clean up)?

Response: Union rules prohibit technical workers from performing cleaning duties and the supervisor of the janitorial staff didn't act on this because he was unaware the floor is dirty.

Question: **Why** (why are such rules tolerated, and why was the supervisor unaware)?

Response: The union rules were recently set, following a large labor dispute. Trying to change them at this time was deemed to not be a politically wise move considering the current state of management / union relations. Also, the janitorial supervisor manages from his desk and rarely gets out in the workplace to see what his staff is doing.

Now choose the answer for the best long-term effect: Sweep the floor? Or, make your expectations clear to the janitorial supervisor and deal with the union issues?

A NOTE OF CAUTION

A number of organizations that are more progressive in pursuing performance improvements have come to frequently applying this concept of asking "Why?" multiple times. This is primarily true in the nuclear power generation business. However, optimum value of the exercise is still often not achieved because the exercise is done perfunctorily and lacks the rigor to ensure that each question of Why? is logically answered and answered in a way that provides value.

FOLLOW-UP

As a young officer in the US Nuclear Submarine Force many years ago, I had the opportunity to serve for a number of years in a shipyard environment, both building and testing nuclear submarines and later overhauling them. This, even more fortunately for me, occurred during the time when Admiral Rickover ran the U.S. naval nuclear program. A human being with higher expectations for excellence in every regard never lived. I was continually impressed with, and actually feared, when one of his inspectors, hand selected by the Admiral himself, would come to me as the responsible officer on a submarine in either construction or overhaul and ask about some seemingly innocuous item, like a small screw he had found lying loose in one of the sub's compartments that contained reactor components. A modern day executive, who has not had the opportunity to grow under the tutelage of a system designed by such a demanding taskmaster as the Admiral, if he found himself in the same situation, might say to the inspector: Look buddy, I'm running a multimillion dollar project here. I'm focusing on strategic issues. I have major problems to worry about. The lives of over a hundred sailors rely on the successful completion of this project. I have a schedule that must be met for the national security of the nation -- and you're asking me about a screw??? But the wiser man would know that the source of the question had to be considered. The Admiral's inspector had likely already completed or would soon complete a review that would find that the screw had fallen out of a piece of equipment that was vital to the safe operation of the nuclear plant in that sub; and that a preventive maintenance item had existed for some time to ensure the tightness of the screw; and that records showed that this particular preventive maintenance item had been performed within the last few days; and that if the preventive maintenance had indeed been properly performed, then the screw would not have been loose; and that the person who had performed that preventive maintenance item had not participated in the training and qualification that was required before a person could work on the subject equipment; and that this individual had also performed the preventive maintenance on a number of other pieces of safety-related equipment; and that this brought the effectiveness of training and preventive maintenance programs into question; and consequently, the reliability of a number of other important pieces of equipment in the sub's nuclear plant were now in question; and that therefore no other work or testing could continue until the entire preventive maintenance effort and the training and qualification program were reviewed and upgraded to preclude recurrence of these problems; and that this would put the submarine's work weeks if not months behind schedule!

Why was that inspector able to determine all of the above? Because he had engrained in him the principle,

15. *PULL THE STRING*

This is a concept that couples well with that of AACT 13 [Y CUBED], but is broader in application. In general, applying [Y CUBED] will provide insight as to why a particular problem exists and how to correct it. [PULLING THE STRING] leads to the identification of other problems related to the initial problem on which the string is pulled. It has more to do with never being satisfied, with never accepting that "stuff happens," with being absolutely committed to the fact that every thing happens for a reason, and then equally committed to finding not only that reason, but every significant contributing factor and related problem as well. In pursuing these reasons and contributors one will often uncover a more significant problem then originally thought. Said another way, the reasons things happen are often more significant than the things that happen themselves.

The string can be pulled on a problem (or a symptom of a problem that may or may not have yet risen to the problem level) by applying the Why question several times, as already discussed. However, limiting one's self to applying only this concept will often result in leaving valuable information unfound. A good observer who wants to be a better observer would be well advised to focus on improving her skill at pulling the string, for this is among the most valuable of tools in her observation tool kit.

A basic framework to apply in pulling the string is to pursue the following aspects of any problem:

1. BARRIERS
   What barriers were or were not in place that could have prevented the problem. These can be physical barriers, such as signs, or they can be non-physical barriers, such as policies, management involvement, or various means of monitoring that would have detected the problem.

2. TRAINING AND QUALIFICATION
   Were those involved in the problem trained and qualified to do what they were doing when the problem occurred?

3. COMMUNICATIONS
   Who said what to whom?

4. SUPERVISION
    What were supervisors (or managers) doing or not
    doing that may have contributed to the problem?

5. EXPECTATIONS
    Are expectations in place, clearly understood, and
    are they being adhered to?

6. HISTORY
    Has the problem ever happened before and why was
    any action that might have been taken to correct
    that problem not effective?

On many occasions, a problem will not be readily self-
evident, and the good observer will have to be alert for
relatively small and at first seemingly insignificant indications
that a problem might exist. Pulling the string on these
indications will sometimes lead to the most valuable insights.
However, often, after extensive digging and following of
leads as one pulls the string, the observer may hit a dead
end. There will be no problem at the end of the search, and
a lot of time will seem to have been wasted. What should one
do? Find another indication and pull the string on that one.
This is again where the high energy of AACT 2 [ENERGY,
EXPERIENCE, AND EXPOSURE ARE THE REQUISITES
OF A GOOD OBSERVER] comes into play.

The following is a personal experience with pulling the
string:

I was once asked to come into a large production facility,
without much advanced warning, and to give to the owners
any insights that would help them maintain the facility as the
excellent operating organization that it was well known to be.
The cardinal sin of coming in without extensive preparation
would be forgiven in this case because of the short-fused

nature of the request. Upon arrival at the facility, I first went to where the workday would be kicked off -- a morning meeting attended by all of the oncoming workers, and at which a supervisor put out whatever information he thought was warranted. I introduced myself but sat in a corner of the room so as to not be conspicuous. A description of the meeting is described in the following paragraph. I have generalized the description so the reader can more readily associate it with similar activities at the reader's workplace. Read the paragraph carefully and mentally put yourself in my position. Jot down on a piece of paper any impressions that you believe would be useful in accomplishing the task to which I was assigned, i.e., provide insights helpful in maintaining a high level of performance. The meeting went as follows:

The supervisor started the meeting with a "safety thought of the day," during which he reinforced the importance of wearing the proper personal protective equipment when performing certain work. The workers were obviously interested in the information and asked several questions for clarification. Then the current operating conditions of the facility were described by the supervisor in charge. This included the fact that passage through two different doors would be limited due to maintenance on the doors. Alternate travel paths were described. One worker seemed a bit frustrated and commented that "work on the doors should have been scheduled for a different time." He indicated that his frustration was based on the travel limitations, which would make his work for the day more difficult. Two other workers spoke up and supported the need for the door work to be done at this time. Following this discussion, the floor was opened for questions. One worker, who was wearing a brown Tee shirt, said that on the previous workday he had been assigned to perform a job, and the paperwork authorizing the work to be done had the same identification number as two other jobs going on in the same vicinity. He said he thought this was wrong and asked if the supervisor also thought this was not the correct way of controlling the work. The supervisor concurred that this use of the serial numbers was not in accordance with policy. He went on to describe what should have occurred had everything been done properly. The supervisor was quite thorough in his description of the proper use of the system for controlling work and engaged several other workers in the discussion to ensure that his points were well understood. Following this interchange, a short special training session was presented to the workers on how to recognize and deal with heat stress. The outside temperature, considering the humidity level, was the equivalent of 115 degrees Fahrenheit, and consequently a few inside areas of the facility had been measured at 130 degrees. The instructor engaged the workers in dialogue to ensure the precautions to avoid heat stress were understood. One worker somewhat cynically stated his belief that if a job that affected the bottom line (money) needed to get done, management would not tolerate work delays intended to allow cooling periods and prevent heat stress. Several of the vocal worker's peers made some barely intelligible remarks that seemed to indicate they disagreed with his negative view of management's support of personnel safety. The instructor reinforced the point that it is the worker's responsibility to follow the facility procedures for heat stress and to leave the work area should certain conditions and symptoms occur. Before the meeting ended, another supervisor entered the room and briefed the workers on a new process for obtaining tools. During this briefing, one of the workers, wearing a Harley-Davidson baseball cap, called out to the briefing supervisor that he had gone to the tool room to get a particular tool one day earlier in the week and found that all of the twenty-some tools of this type, which are normally stored in the room, had been removed from the tool room and sent off the facility for calibration at the same time. The Harley hat man asked, "Wouldn't it be better if calibration of these tools was staggered since this is a common tool and there is frequently a need for it?" The tool supervisor agreed this would be better, and the meeting ended.

What impressions have you written down and what would you do with any information you acquired in the observation of this meeting? Give this some thought before reading on.

The notes I made on this observation when it happened included the two positive impressions that I would share with management in hope of encouraging continuation of the positive practices: that considerations of personal safety were clearly present in various portions of the meeting; and that an obvious effort had been made (and was successful) to engage the workers in dialogue, both to get any feedback and also to ensure their understanding of key points presented. However, more importantly, I saw the makings of a significant problem in the organization and went about pulling the string on leads I had acquired in my observation.

As part of pulling the string, I subsequently had the following interchange with the Harley Hat Man (HHM):

Me: When you were unable to acquire the tool, which had been taken off for calibration, what was the result? Was there any adverse impact or any consequence?

HHM: Yes, We were working on an important air conditioning unit that has been out of service for several weeks due to other work delays. It won't be long before we reach the limit for the amount of time this unit is allowed to be out of service. After that, we'll have to shut down the facility.

Me: That's a really good point. I suppose with most other tools requiring periodic calibration that they are taken off for calibration in sequential groups so that some of the tools are always available.

HHM: That's correct. Taking all these tools off-site at the same time is crazy.

Me: Did you get the impression from the body language of the tool room supervisor you spoke to in the meeting that he intends to take any action on your comment? I didn't see him taking any notes?

HHM: (Laughing) No.

Me: The site has a process by which whenever a problem is identified, like the one you pointed out for example, a form called a Corrective Action Report or CR is written. That CR then gets assigned to the appropriate manager for corrective action. The form is also tracked to ensure the action is taken and the problem is not likely to recur. Are you aware of the process? Have you ever had training on how to submit one of these CRs?

HHM: Yeah.

Me: Is this the kind of problem for which you should submit a CR ?

HHM: Yeah

Me: Well why wouldn't you submit it? You have a really important job and it's a shame to see your kind of talent held up from doing work by a simple glitch in a system that takes all of your tools away.

HHM: I guess I've gotten in the habit of just telling someone about problems.

Me: Well thanks for your time. I appreciate your being candid with me. I'm just trying to see what can be done to make your job around here easier and safer. Good luck to you. I may need to call you again if I have more questions. I hope you won't mind.

HHM: No problem.

I had the following interchange with the supervisor who led the meeting:

Me: Nice job on the meeting. It's good to see such interest in personal safety. I noticed that HHM and Mr. Brown Tee (I actually used their real first names) brought up what seemed to me to be some really valid issues that either slow down the process of getting work done or that could cause other problems with the proper control and documentation of the work. Did I understand these correctly?

Supervisor in Charge (SIC): (Described in great detail, each of the problems that occurred, with both the unavailability of the tools and the wrong use of the serial numbers used to control work in the case of Mr. Brown Tee. He clearly understood what had happened in each case and that they were problems.)

Me: HHM told me that his issue with the tools caused the work on that air conditioning unit to be held up again. Is that what happened?

SIC: Yeah. (He then went on to tell me what a "nightmare" it has been trying to get the air conditioning job done with all of the work delays.)

Me: I'm curious as to why a CR wasn't submitted on either of those two problems. Whose responsibility would that be anyway? You as the supervisor? Or are the workers themselves supposed to submit the CR?

SIC: Either the supervisor or the worker can submit the CR. We expect whoever identifies the problem to submit the CR. I guess we didn't submit them because we just didn't think about it.

I then resorted to my most valuable assessment tool -- a pizza. I bought several pizzas and invited a group of workers to sit down for an open discussion. I was up front about my assignment at the facility and reinforced that whatever could be done to improve the great job they were already doing would be in their best interest. They agreed and were very supportive, and like most people at the worker level, had nothing to hide.

I asked the workers a wide range of questions since I had the opportunity to interact with them. Among the questions was whether or not they typically write CRs when they find a problem. They candidly told me they would usually not write a CR. When I pursued why, they told me in great detail about all the extra work that resulted for them from writing a CR, including the fact that the person who writes the CR is expected to be the one who finds an "owner" for the CR (someone responsible for fixing the problem identified in the CR). Several of them offered that this extra work is "definitely not worth the effort," since when a CR is written "nothing usually happens" and the problem remains uncorrected.

I added a note, "writing CRs" to a 3X5 card I typically carry in my pocket and used this as a reminder to ask questions similar to the above to whatever other workers I might interact with. I did ask the question, and the majority of the responses were similar.

Now knowing that problems in implementing the process for getting work done at this facility were not being reported in the system that would ensure those problems got corrected, I wanted to get a feel for whether or not there was any higher level <u>result</u> or <u>consequence</u> of this problem. So I went to the location where all work is approved prior to starting, and I observed for a while. Within an hour I had seen six instances of the work management process not being adhered to. In questioning those approving the work I found that at least four of the instances I observed were frequent occurrences. (I also found that the work start approver also did not typically write CRs, but chose instead to write problems down on a piece of scrap paper and turn them over to the person who relieved him for the backshift.)

I concluded at this point that there were significant problems in implementation of the work management process and that these problems were not being reported and corrected. This could have had a direct impact on safety, since an other than smooth flow of work resulted in work delays and in needed equipment being out of service for repairs longer than necessary. I had also developed insight into <u>why</u> the problems were not being corrected. With this information I was still not satisfied. I assumed, as I always do, that the managers at this facility were very capable and well intentioned, and I did not understand why they would not have already seen and acted on this problem. Said another way, what management barriers to the problem were there and why were they not working? I examined the barriers that would typically exist in any organization: management monitoring through use of indicators, their personal observations in the workplace, and their use of the internal oversight organization. A brief description of how I examined and what I found with each of these barriers follows:

Oversight group

I invited the person in the oversight organization respon-sible for looking at the management of work to come along with me while I observed activities in the area where work was approved to start. This gent was candid and anxious to learn, and I soon discovered that pulling the string and focusing on results or consequences were not his strengths. He shared with me that he had recently looked at the work management process and found it to be "sound with no problems." His lack of exposure as discussed in AACT 2 [EXPERIENCE, ENER-GY, AND EXPOSURE ARE THE REQUISITES OF A GOOD OBSERVER] was a key contributor to the difficulties he was having in identifying existing problems in areas he assessed.

Management observations in the workplace

These observations were not happening. I asked several of the workers when was the last time they had seen a manager out in the workplace. That answer was considerably negative. Several also commented that managers don't understand the magnitude of the problems the workers deal with because they don't have to deal with the problems.

Indicators

Problems such as those discussed above would typically be evident in an indicator of how frequently changes are made to the work schedule. Simply stated, a job gets delayed because of some reason, such as a tool is not available, and that job cannot be worked as scheduled. Rather than have the workers sit around, a different job, and one not originally planned for, is assigned at the last minute. The resulting turmoil in the schedule causes no end of grief for the workers who are trying to plan for and conduct the work. I thought surely the managers must be monitoring this important indicator -- and they were! And the number for schedule stability was great! It indicated that more than 90 percent of the scheduled work was completed as scheduled! I was wrong! Or was I? I continued to pull the string.

As I dug into the numbers that went to make up the schedule stability picture, I found that indeed over 90 percent of the scheduled work was completed as scheduled. However, most of the "work" that was included in calculations of this schedule indicator was in fact not "work." It was periodically recurring tests and checks, which for this facility are required by federal law to be performed as scheduled. When non-repetitive, non-legally required maintenance activities, such as the type I had observed, were broken out of the overall numbers, and schedule stability was recalculated, it was closer to 30%! This meant that if 100 jobs were assigned to be done within a particular time, only 30 of those jobs would actually get started, and even fewer would get done.

I developed the following conclusions:

- Works schedule stability at this organization was poor (among the lowest in this particular industry, based on comparisons I made).

- A range of deficiencies with implementation and monitoring of the work management process was observed, and these were contributing to the problem of schedule instability.

- Managers were not aware of these deficiencies because they didn't often get out into the workplace to observe or interact with the workers.

- The process which is typically used to identify and correct problems of this type (use of CRs) was not being used.

I also had another string to pull -- how broad was the problem of managers not knowing what was going on in their areas of responsibility. This was a string I would pull later.

My above conclusions and insights resulted simply because I took note of some innocuous comments that were made in an otherwise unexciting shop meeting and then PULLED THE STRING.

BE A DOUBTING THOMAS

The average person hearing the name Ronald Reagan would likely not immediately recognize it as being that of the purveyor of good observation techniques. Yet our fortieth president did provide us with at least one highly effective observation tool. Although the following words were, to some degree, crafted by Condileeza Rice for Ronald Reagan, it was he who used them in the course of his discussions with the Soviets a number of years ago. His words were specifically related to the control of nuclear weapons. He told his esteemed Soviet counterpart that of course he trusted him, but "trust but verify" would be his operating principle. "Trust but verify" is a great technique for an observer. People rarely lie; however, they often say things that are untrue, either because they were misinformed, or they misheard, or they didn't really know. So rather than appear unknowledgeable, they guess, and with the regularity inherent in nature's random way, they guess wrong. The point here is to listen to what people have to say, but then,

16. *GO SEE FOR YOURSELF*

Early one morning, while walking around a production facility, I noticed that required precautions had not been taken to ensure that an important pump was available if it should be needed. One method of ensuring reliability in this particular facility was to have redundancy for important pieces of equipment like this pump. This was normally accomplished by taking special precautions, including posting of signs, barriers, and special instructions, to ensure that whenever one of a pair of these pumps was taken out of service for maintenance, the remaining pump remained undisturbed and therefore readily available. In the case at hand, these signs and instructions had not been posted. I reported this to the supervisor responsible, who acknowledged the error and informed me he would quickly remedy the situation. I went back to the components late that evening, about five hours after I had reported the problem, and noted that the signs were still not in place. I estimated, conservatively, that their posting should have taken about forty-five minutes, allowing for all of the approvals and for accessing the area. I then reported this continuing deficient state, along with reference to my earlier report, to the next manager up the chain of seniority. My hosts were quite embarrassed to hear this and quickly scrambled to get the proper precautions posted -- as their internal procedures required. Early the next day, the responsible manager went well out of his way to track me down and again thank me for identifying the deficient condition and to inform me that the appropriate signs, barriers, and instructions were now in place. Although the subject components were not in a readily accessible area, I ignored the considerable inconvenience to myself, donned the special clothing needed to access the area where the signs were to be posted, and again took the time to go back to the components and see the signs for myself. I also asked one of the workers at the facility to go with me, wanting to ensure the clarity of the postings from the view of those for whom the signs were intended. We found that indeed the signs had been placed, but not on all of the components. One very important component had been missed in hanging the signage. Also, the signs that were posted were sloppily posted with masking tape. One had already fallen down and was lying on the floor in the area. When I noticed that the signs had been hand written and the wording on the signs differed from each other when they should have been the same, I asked the accompanying worker what the wording on each of the signs meant to him and what was his understanding of the restrictions indicated on the signs. He readily shared his confusion with the different wording on the various signs. Needless to say that when I reported these latest observations to the previously embarrassed manager, not only was he two-fold more embarrassed, but also, hopefully, he recognized that trust but verify, or GO SEE FOR YOURSELF, is a good technique, applicable to many situations.

REMINDER NOTES

Another technique that I have used effectively over the years and that I have never seen any other use or adaptation of by any other person or organization has to do with a small piece of paper. I consider it so important I would not do an assessment or observation of any type if I was prohibited, for whatever reason, from using it. Again, the technique is basic. It would sound a lot more impressive if I were to launch into a technical jargon-laden monologue on computer applications and use of technology and data-bases to identify issues and trends. However, the fact is that I have never seen weak observations made stronger solely by the use of technology. So rather than suggesting you go out and buy a palmtop or a laptop, let me suggest that you go out and buy, and then,

17. USE 3X5 CARDS

Of course, I say this only somewhat facetiously, and more to make a point on the importance of preparing with reminder notes in any effort intended to collect information.

It is not the 3X5 card itself, but rather the way it is used that is important. Although I must say, that, personally, I feel as strongly about the specific use of 3X5 cards as any other piece of writing medium because I have found them so useful over the years. Their size, which allows a handy fit into a shirt pocket, facilitates the most valuable aspect of their use -- always readily at hand, to add notes or to refer to when an opportunity arises to ask a question.

Well before you visit any organization for an observation, have an agreed-to agenda for meeting with people within the organization. In the same early time frame, you need to have already started laying out topics for discussion with each individual with whom you will meet. At least one, and often more than one, 3X5 card should be designated for each individual, and should contain some key words or phrases as reminder notes to outline topics or points of discussion. None of these topics or points should cover "gray" information as described in AACT 12 [IGNORE THE GRAY INFORMATION]. Examples of such gray information-targeted comments applicable here would include: Describe your organization, and, explain how this or that process works. Rather they are to be evaluative topics or points that you should have extracted from extensive preparation efforts. Sitting on a plane and reading a report, or walking through a factory, hospital, or other facility, often brings questions to mind such as, why would a manager tolerate some condition you observe, or what are the manager's expectations for performance of an activity that looks to be performed to a substandard level. These notes can then be jotted down on that manager's 3X5 card for later discussion.

The handy list of discussion points also allows prioritization of the discussion items in the event a manager becomes available for discussion but has limited time. Furthermore, having the list handy allows getting in an extra question or two should you cross paths with the manager in a hallway or at lunch.

The following is an example of a 3X5 card that I have actually used in an observation, along with more complete descriptions of what each note reminder would mean to me as well as some background information. Note that, as indicated in the explanatory notes following each question, I had developed background information related to each discussion topic, with each item having a performance basis.

NOTES FOR DISCUSSION WITH SENIOR EXECUTIVE OF A LARGE HEALTHCARE FACILITY

- SAFETY NOT IN MISSION? Complete question: *I noticed that the term "safety" is not used in either your mission or vision. What is your thinking on that? (Discussions with other workers and managers had already indicated that they had no understanding that safety was the top priority of this executive, as it was indicated to be in other company literature.)*

- TOP 3 FOCUS? Complete question: *What are your top 3 focus areas for the organization? (I intended to then test the communication of these top priorities down through the organization to determine if people are really focused on the things on which the executive expects them to focus.)*

- EXPECTATIONS RE. LAST OBSERVATION? Complete question: *What do you expect your employees to have done to correct the problems that were identified in the last review of your facility? (I had already determined that some of the problems identified in the last review remained unchanged, and that no manager to date had*

been able to discuss either the last review report or any
actions to address issues from the last report.)

HOW MONITOR PERFORMANCE? Complete question:
How, other than through use of the quantitative indicators that
I saw in your business plan, do you monitor to ensure you know
what is going on in your facilities? (I had already observed a
number of poor practices in the workplace and heard remarks
that managers essentially are never seen in the field. On the rare
occasions when they were seen in the work place, they typically did
not react to any inappropriate practices which were going on at
the time.

THE MAGIC STONE

I don't know the source of the following fairy tale but would
be glad to give credit for it if I did. I heard it many years ago
when it was told by a nuclear executive who was one of many
of my unknowing mentors. I convey it here to the best of my
recollection because it relates well to the next AACT.

Once there was a farmer whose farm was doing poorly.
Little money was coming in from the milk provided by his
small herd of cows. His chickens had stopped laying eggs
some time ago and the revenue from egg sales was at its lowest
point ever. The cost of diesel fuel for his tractor had risen and
usage of the fuel was higher than it had been in some time.
The farm seemed to be falling apart. The fence around his
property had collapsed in several areas and lay in disrepair. His
two workmen just did not seem able to keep up with all of the
maintenance required on the fences, the tractor, and the farm
buildings. One day as the poor farmer sat in his little house
lamenting his lot, a beautiful fairy appeared and offered him
any single wish of his choice. Without hesitation he wished
for his little farm to be prosperous. The fairy handed him a

small, shiny black stone; told him it was a magic stone; and then said: Take this stone and carry it to each of the farthest corners of your farm. After you have completed this task your farm will be prosperous. The farmer considered this to be nonsense, but having nothing to lose, accepted the stone and marched off to the first of the most remote corners of his farm. Shortly before he reached the corner he crossed a small field where he found his tractor running idle as a worker took a short and well-deserved break for some lunch and water. The farmer stopped the engine of the tractor and told the worker that he expected the tractor to be running only when in use. He then proceeded on to the corner, where nothing happened. The farmer put aside his disappointment and set off for the next remote corner, taking a shortcut through his hen yard. As he passed through the yard he came upon a raccoon exiting a small hole in the wire fence surrounding the yard. Dripping from the raccoon's mouth were the remains of one or more fresh eggs. The farmer chased away the raccoon, quickly repaired the hole in the fence, and again moved on. Before he had gone very far he saw in the distance one of his cows that was obviously ready to be milked, but that had wandered off onto a neighbor's land. Grumbling to himself, he led the cow back onto his property, made a mental note to have one of his workers milk the cow that afternoon and establish a schedule for future milkings. He repositioned the fallen fence post over which the cow had stepped to escape, and moved on to the second corner -- where again nothing happened. He was now convinced he had been duped by the supposed fairy. But his farm had one more remote corner and he, with little faith, moved on toward it. When he got to the corner, again nothing happened. As he was about to leave and return to his house he noticed that one of his workman was soundly asleep among a huge pile of fallen leaves. He angrily woke the worker, told him in no uncertain terms what would happen if he was found sleeping on the job again, and then stomped off toward the house. When he arrived at the house he threw the stone into the woods and regretted his foolishness for ever having believed it was magic. As time passed and days turned into weeks, the farmer noticed that his tractor fuel bills had been slowly going down. His workers were finding more eggs from the hens. The money coming in from milk sales began to slowly rise. And the farm even began to look better, with the workers now seeming able to get more done. The fences had gotten repaired, the farm sheds were painted and the grass was neatly mowed. The farmer was now happy but had no idea why his farm was doing so much better. Somewhere a fairy was smiling.

Executives unfamiliar with the above fairy tale often visit other organizations to get ideas, or to informally benchmark. They sometimes make these visits as a favor to the head of the visited organization, in order to share their views of the conditions and performance of the organization. This is a good idea and these visits in their purest sense are a form of assessment. Unfortunately, many of these executives either do not get an accurate picture of the visited organization, or have good gut impressions, but lack the objective information to convey a compelling point to the host or hostess of their visit. Why? Because they don't do as the farmer with the magic stone did and get into the remote corners of the farm, that is, they don't

18. *GET IN THE TRENCHES*

Things only happen in the trenches, where the workers go -- the remote areas of a plant, factory, healthcare facility (or farm); the places that are hard to get to, that are hot and uncomfortable, or that require wearing special types of clothing or protective equipment; the types of places not seen on a VIP tour; places that aren't waxed and buffed or just walked down prior to the VIP's arrival. If the visited organization has problems with performance or conditions, it is in these prime places where they will occur. (Keep this in mind the next time you read the comments of some Senator visiting a military base or some other politician visiting an entire country.) A side benefit of getting into some of these more remote areas is that the workers will respect someone who makes the effort to come into their environment. They typically don't often see the "suits" in these areas. As an observer, your interest in what the workers do will open them up more to discussion. They'll tell you things you will need to know to get an accurate picture of what is really happening in an organization. Workers are never reluctant to talk about problems that they have to deal with on a daily basis.

I was once asked to come into an organization and validate senior management's conclusions that they had made extensive gains in reducing worker errors by a strong push on procedural compliance. Upon arrival, I chose to bypass their formal presentation on the actions taken to improve this area and the initiative that drove it. Instead, I went directly to a classroom where new employees receive their initial training and orientation to the facility. I noted that the practical demonstration of how to use site safety equipment was not conducted, even though required by the lesson plan; a number of poor practices, which were contrary to procedures, were essentially reinforced because they were observed but not corrected by the instructors; and the instructors were unaware of senior management's strong emphasis and recent focus on procedural compliance. These trainers, even though they play such a vital role in the formative stages of new employees by being the first to interact with them, were inadvertently left out of the improvement initiative. Had I not gone into the trenches and seen this myself (even without my magic stone), it likely would have never come to light.

Be cautioned that this sequence of performing an assessment by first getting out into the work area is not an easy action in itself. Any manager who knows someone is going to be observing in his area will want to show the observer his plans or discuss his intentions. He will want to talk about what he has accomplished and how far he has come in his effort. All of this information can be useful, but will be even more useful if viewed with an understanding of what is actually occurring in the trenches -- today. Using this approach, you may be amazed to find how little of what those at the top say their organizations are doing, is actually either happening, or even understood by the workers to have been expected to happen.

TRACKING SKILL

Anyone who is an outdoors person will readily acknowledge that if you want to find out if a particular creature frequents some area, you cannot accomplish this by relying on seeing that creature during your visits to that area. Regardless of how frequently a creature visits a place, the likelihood of a sighting opportunity is small and heavily dependent on luck. The odds, of course, change if one has studied its habits and patiently waits the creature out. An effective observer does not have the time to wait when the creature in question is a manager and the area of interest is the workplace. So outdoor logic leads us to the conclusion that if you want to find out if managers frequent the workplace (as they should in order to set and reinforce their expectations, with or without the magic stone), then one should,

19. *LOOK FOR "MANAGEMENT TRACKS"*

Visits to the trenches, as discussed above, will provide the added opportunity to look for management tracks.

One can't truly assess an organization without forming

a judgment regarding the effectiveness of management in that organization. On a short-term observation, only on infrequent occasions will one have a chance to actually see managers doing their jobs, in the workplace, with the workers. Typically, limitations of time will not support this opportunity. Consequently, it's important to try not only to observe management, but to also observe the effects of management, or, as referred to here, management tracks. These tracks are various signs and forms of evidence that managers have been in the area. They can take the form of people being able to articulate what management wants or what management's standards are; comments that indicate management has been in the area recently and/or interacted with the workers; a familiarity of the workforce with the managers; conditions that reflect the expectations that the managers have said they set. The approach of getting in the trenches and looking for management tracks is so effective in observation that it should typically be the first thing one does upon arriving at an organization for observation purposes. This approach also allows one to form a judgment regarding what is really happening in an organization before being biased by the lofty plans and intentions of the senior managers, and by what they hope is happening in their organizations.

INFORMATION PROCESSING

As one goes about an observation, either structured or unstructured, an incredible amount of information will be acquired. I have already discussed culling out the gray information, but how does one deal with all of the black and the white information?

20. CONTINUALLY FORM HYPOTHESES AND THEN PROVE OR DISPROVE THEM

To work fast in the world of assessment, get in the habit

of forming conclusions quickly, and on limited information. Some will argue with this approach. Those are the people you will find floundering in a sea of information who will be unable to arrive at a conclusion regardless of how much information is collected. Remember that the price of perfect motion is total immobility. If you want to make something "perfect," whether it's a motion you're performing, an object you're making, or a document you're writing, you're on the wrong track. You can strive for perfection but you'll never get there. Consequently, if you have perfection as a criterion for final production, your product will never see market. So don't look for the perfect conclusion with an uncountable number of irrefutable examples. Wisdom is the ability to draw conclusions with limited information, and wisdom comes from experience. Remember AACT 2 [EXPERIENCE, EXPOSURE, AND ENERGY ARE THE REQUISITES OF A GOOD OBSERVER]. Experience is the fundamental trait that applies here. Right from the start, force yourself to draw conclusions as soon as you have any reasonable amount of information. If you walk around a facility and you hear several people blaming each other for some problem that happened in the facility, you have the makings of a hypothesis: There is a lack of teamwork in the organization. When moving on to collect other information and to look at other areas, keep that hypothesis in mind -- and in your notes. Take note of anything that either disproves or proves the hypothesis. At the conclusion of the observation, if you have done an adequate job, you will have enough information to easily make the decision on whether or not it was a valid hypothesis. Again, if you are putting out the mental effort that a good observation requires, you will have numerous hypotheses. Your experience, along with feedback from the staff being observed will tell you what the more important hypotheses are. You will also need to prioritize your efforts and your conclusions. More about prioritization later.

Although it may at first seem to not be the case, another key to dealing with the large amount of information that is available in any observation is,

21. *WRITE DOWN EVERYTHING*

This, of course, assumes one has already applied AACT 12 [IGNORE THE GRAY INFORMATION]. Information at the black and white ends of the information spectrum often has greater meaning in the context of other information acquired at different times. As an observer, think of yourself as a person putting together a jigsaw puzzle that will eventually and pictorially describe the performance of the organization you are observing. Think of the last time you put a jigsaw puzzle together. How many of the pieces of the puzzle made sense or conveyed a clear part of a picture by themselves? Similarly, what would the final picture of an organization look like if the observer, particularly in the early stages, discards pieces that don't, by themselves, provide a meaningful picture? For example, a seemingly valueless comment later considered in the context of other information can add to the clarity of an important picture. An executive in charge of a large technical facility once told me that he was unsure of the status of a training program for the engineers in his organization. By itself, this bit of information is little more than somewhat interesting, but certainly seems not to be significant, considering all of the many things on the plate of an executive like this who has such a broad range of responsibilities. I later found out that just a month earlier, a regulatory agency had threatened to remove the certification of this particular training program --an action that would have significantly impacted the production of the facility. A similar threat to the certification had also arisen two years earlier. In both of the latter cases, a lack of involvement in the training program by senior management at the facility had been cited as a contributing factor. This later acquired information put a totally different complexion on the original expression of ignorance.

Some will argue that writing everything down is not necessary; that intelligent and experienced people will retain the important information in their memories. Don't believe it. Uncountable numbers of very experienced and very capable executives with whom I have had the pleasure of working retained very little of the information they received early in an observation. They consequently tended to make judgments based solely on the most recently acquired information. This should not be surprising, because typically the initial information gathered is new, digested for only a short period of time, and is followed by a continuing stream of other new information. An empirical curve of an amount of memorized information plotted against time would show an exponential decrease in retention over time. This shortfall in the retention capabilities of the typical human being is a good reason to rewrite your rough notes directly following an interview or activity observation. This helps to ensure that you capture clearly not only what you wrote in shorthand during the observation, but also the impressions that passed through your mind as things were observed and as both spoken and unspoken messages were exchanged during an interview.

Writing everything down isn't easy. It takes effort. It also takes the practiced skill of writing one thing while listening to another, and continuing to politely maintain at least the appearance of attention to what another is saying while writing. This point again goes back to AACT 2 [EXPERIENCE, EXPOSURE, AND ENERGY ARE THE REQUISITE ATTRIBUTES OF A GOOD OBSERVER]. It takes a person of high energy to put out the full effort required to effectively capture in notes the results of an observation.

I have long found that steno notebooks are handy for keeping notes, although any paper will do. Also, massive amounts of information can be grouped and analyzed with a personal computer. However, to keep on the point of the technique at hand, which is to "record" everything, I will continue with my tendency to keep things simple and encourage use of good old fashioned handwriting. Writing the information in one notebook allows early and useful cataloguing and categorization of the information. Typically, in addition to the black and white information, as described in AACT12 [IGNORE THE GRAY INFORMATION] occasions will arise when the observer needs to also record items that require follow-up by the observer. I have found as a useful technique, to simply mark a "plus" sign beside any piece of information that is noted positively, whether it is the condition of an item or the comment of an individual. An open "block" annotated next to a written note would be used to highlight an item that requires follow-up. You may be surprised that such cataloguing of information allows you to quickly skim your notes and begin forming early impressions and hypotheses that are based on solid observations rather than gut feelings. Gut feelings are conclusions that experienced people come to when they cannot recall the basis for the impressions they have formed. An observer, whose effectiveness will be gauged by the amount of insightful detail he provides to his customer at the conclusion of his observation, does not have the luxury of not recalling the bases of his conclusions.

MORE USE OF MAGIC

After collecting a large amount of information, the next step is to borrow from the books of magic and the superstitions linked to that common drink, tea, and symbolically,

22. *STIR THE TEA LEAVES*

The practice of stirring tea leaves and then looking into them to see a story of the future unfolding is a technique used by wizards long in the past. But it works! It works if it's applied in practical terms -- to observation data. The tea leaves of the observer are the facts and impressions he has gathered. These "tea leaves" also tell a story, but only to the eye experienced enough to read them, and only when configured in certain ways. Thus the need for stirring. This is analogous to the importance of sorting the information one has collected in various ways until it provides not only the most accurate, but also the most compelling, picture of the organization or activity being assessed. Like the magical tea leaves, this data could indeed indicate the future of that organization.

As a most straightforward example, consider the white or particularly positive information one might have recorded. This type of information typically requires the least sorting or rearranging or stirring of the tea leaves. If annotated in such a way that it is easily reviewed in composite, it can quickly give a first view of the fundamental strengths of an organization. For example, if after a day with an organization, the white information list consists of only a few narrowly defined practices or a listing of very non-results-oriented generalities, then the tea leaves say that this is at best a mediocre organization and it is not likely headed in the right direction. Examples of the former would include the clear format of some report, or the usefulness of a newly acquired piece of equipment. Examples of the latter would include the "friendliness of the employees," or the "interest of management in doing the right thing," (which is one of those things observers usually say when they have nothing else nice to say).

Stirring the tea leaves of the black information may result in the identification of an underlying problem that was not evident in any one observation item by itself. For example, if observations of the performance of caregivers in a healthcare facility include shortfalls in consistently cleansing their hands when required, performing the proper patient identification checks, and using required precautions to preclude patient falls, there may be a commonality among these items. Follow-up would be needed to verify any of these, but potential commonalities include lack of the existence or clarity of policies governing these as well as other activities, gaps in caregiver indoctrination and training, and the ineffectiveness of supervisory presence on the nursing floors.

An important point related to the above discussion is that black information can be grouped in a number of different ways as the tea leaves are stirred. It is useful to consider each note of observation as a symptom of a problem rather than as a problem in itself. Then, group these symptoms and discard any groupings that have the relatively fewest number of items in them. What remain will be sound conclusions, the basis of which will be as strong as the examples in the groupings. One caution when grouping this information is to retain only those groupings with at least three or more supporting notes or observations. Human nature is such that at least one of your notes will be disputable and with two or fewer examples, the point will be weakly supported or possibly invalid. If such is the case your credibility will suffer. This is an extremely shortened description of a topic on symptom classification that warrants more time than can be afforded in this discussion.

Before leaving this topic, one final example of how the technique of stirring the tea leaves can provide value follows. A sufficient number of observations at any hospital's intensive care unit might yield a wide range of facts related to the use of alarms. These alarms are used to monitor vital patient information and to alert caregivers to the need for immediate attention. The observations might include instances of alarms that were not responded to for varying periods of time, and for varying reasons. Some of these alarms would likely be more important than others, and this also would be noted in the observations. There may as well be observations of other shortfalls related to the use of alarms, but not necessarily in the category of alarm response. Stirring the tea leaves, or configuring and reconfiguring the detailed observations in order to understand the bigger picture of performance in this case, and to formulate the most useful message for the management in charge of the unit, could result in a concise message that will have an impact. The following is an example: "Numerous instances were observed in which patient alarms were not responded to. Several of these alarms warned of potentially lethal heart problems, one of which was not responded to for 45 minutes. Additionally, the audible signal on one of the alarms was silenced by a unit secretary for the reason, as she described it, "to reduce the noise level on the unit." This is certainly a more effective way to convey the collected information than to dump on the manager in charge a large set of seemingly unrelated facts, each of varying importance.

AVOIDING GOSSIP

Occasions will arise when it is very tempting to report what someone said. For example, I recall one assessment report from an internal oversight organization that, among its findings, had the statement, "Supervisors said that the volume of information provided to them as required reading is excessive." My advice is, go ahead and report things like this -- if you want to be little more than a messenger; if you want to be like a pollster or like those consultants who lack experience and therefore do little more than report what people have said. But be sure you are right even in this reporting. Is that <u>exactly</u> what the supervisors said? Did they do it with a certain amount of inflection in their voices that might indicate they were saying it facetiously? Did they exhibit body language that indicated there was more in the message than their words? What gauge or criteria were used to determine "excessive"? And is what they said really what they meant? When they complained about the required reading, were they really conveying that they disagree with the concept of having required reading? Were they trying to make a point that they just don't like their boss? Such are the questions that pollsters need not worry about. What a top-shelf observer would do relative to this information is,

23. *REPORT JUDGMENT, NOT HEARSAY*

A seasoned observer takes in what everyone who has spoken has said, including what they "said" with gestures and inflection as well as words; factors in other observations he has made; includes a heavy dose of what the various statements and observations mean, based on his previous experience; and draws a conclusion based on his judgment of all this information. In other words, don't just report that Joe said there is a problem; report that there is or is not a problem (in your judgment), what's causing the problem, and what might be done to fix it.

It needs to be recognized that there is a certain amount of risk involved here. It is a simple and risk-free task to report only what Joe said, but an observer's reputation and credibility rest on the accuracy of what she reports. When she makes a judgment, it better be right. On the other hand, just reporting what Joe said is also not fail-safe, even if that information is accurate. There is a reasonable probability that when asked (and under actual or perceived threat), Joe will say that he never said what was reported. Overall, the best approach is to report what your assessment, flavored by your experience, indicates. Don't limit yourself to being only a messenger.

THE SOLUTION AS AN ASPECT OF PROBLEMS

Years ago, in the Submarine Force, while stationed on an older submarine, I received an inspection of my submarine by a highly technically oriented group within the Navy organization. The inspection findings included the startling finding that the passageways on the submarine were three-quarters of an inch narrower than the dimension called for in the design plans of the vessel. It was also noted that this non-adherence to the submarine design specifications had no operational impact on the submarine. I marveled at the uselessness of this finding, but it stuck with me throughout the years and eventually led me to an axiom that was a key part of my observation tool chest:

24. *IF YOU HAVEN'T CONSIDERED THE SOLUTION, YOU HAVEN'T FULLY CONSIDERED THE PROBLEM*

In the example above, there was no solution, especially considering the age of the vessel. Consequently, the finding was of no use to us on the sub. Had the inspector looked at the possible solutions to the problem he would have concluded that outside of rebuilding the submarine, there was no solution to the problem, and that this was tolerable because there were really no negative repercussions as a result of the problem. Consequently, one could argue, there was no problem. In fact, application of AACT 11 [SO WHAT?] would have aborted this illegitimate problem at birth. In a more recent example, I once worked with a team of observers who identified that a schedule for completion of a project was not achievable as currently being worked. It wasn't until the team brainstormed the possible solutions that we determined a lot more information needed to be gathered before even we fully understood the problem, let alone were knowledgeable enough of it to present it to our customer in a useful way. This included finding out what the productivity rates were, what the biggest barrier to productivity was, who was aware of the small likelihood of achieving the current schedule and what was being done about it, as well as a host of other information elements.

A NOTE OF CAUTION: Many problems are complex and difficult to solve. More then one observer has fallen into the trap of sympathy, and without even recognizing what he was doing, dropping pursuit of a problem because he himself could not come up with a solution to it. He had essentially concluded the problem unsolvable. All problems are solvable and it would be a disservice to the assessment customer to not bring a problem to his attention assuming that because you cannot come up with a solution that neither will he.

CHAPTER 4
READING, LISTENING, AND WATCHING

Observing to assess involves three fundamental activities: reading documents, talking (and more importantly listening) to people, and watching activities. The quality of assessment is then determined not only by the selection of targets to which these activities are applied, but equally if not more importantly, by the techniques applied to the reading, listening, and watching. A good observer will read more in a document than is contained in the written words, will hear more than is spoken, and will see as much in actions that are not performed as in those that are.

READING

It is important to understand that the points described below are in regard to reading <u>during the on-site assessment or observation.</u> During the preparation phase, when time availability is less a luxury than it is during the hectic pace of an assessment, the goal should be to read everything the observer can get her hands on. The more the observer knows about the organization, the more meaningful will be what is observed. Once the observer is at the facility and in the process of observing and assessing, then the entire focus needs to be on acquiring the most valuable information. This is not the time to be doing the reading that should have been done in the preparatory phase. It is the time to which the following advice pertains.

One first has to determine what kind of documents should be read. It may be easier to first say what kind of documents should not be read in the course of an observation, primarily because the reading of these is not the most effective use of time. Ironically, these are the documents that most observers first look at -- procedures and plans.

Procedures are replete with gray information. One can save considerable time by only reviewing procedures describing how work is to be done, after watching work to see how it is actually done, and for follow-up on specific questions.

Plans are not worth reviewing unless one is "fishing" because he doesn't know where else to look. Plans, as mentioned earlier, are just promises; in some cases, hopes -- they are often nothing more than what people want to do. Once again, plans that describe what is going to be done can provide insight after observing what is being done, supposedly in accordance with the plan.

25. *THE MOST INFORMATIVE DOCUMENTS ARE THOSE THAT CONTAIN "EVALUATIVE" INFORMATION*

Evaluative information is that which allows one to discern between what is good and what is not good. The "black" and "white" information discussed under AACT12 [IGNORE THE GRAY INFORMATION] is a subset of evaluative information.

Other such information includes metrics or indicators, which will be discussed below in more detail, and any reports of self-assessment activities, such as management observations, event reports, or year-end rollups of performance-related information.

The most important aspects to look for in evaluative information are to what degree the content of such information is critical and candid, and whether or not the information indicates attention to the <u>performance of people</u>, rather than just physical conditions or process-related information. Organizations that are not performing well are in such a state because of what people are or are not doing. Consequently, actions to improve organizational performance, if they are to have any effect, must cause people to change their performance. If oversight reports don't address the performance of people, then logic indicates that the subsequent corrective actions won't either. People performance won't change and neither will that of the organization. The following is an actual and classic example of reluctance to identify people performance issues.

A large, normally well run production facility had to be shutdown for several days, at an expense of several hundred thousand dollars, because of damage to a large production machine. The damage had been caused by a small piece of metal that had fallen into the machine and vibrated against a vital part of the production machine, eventually causing a break in a machine part. Facility management had been aware that the metal piece had fallen into the machine, but allowed the machine to continue operating based on an engineer's conclusion that the metal piece was not as hard as the machine components and thus would cause no damage. In hindsight, it was obvious that the engineer had been wrong in his conclusion. This particular facility had a history of being overly sensitive to the feelings of workers and thus being reluctant to identify and act on issues involving performance. An investigation into the above problem concluded that, "the <u>process </u>by which the engineer had drawn his faulty conclusion was deficient in that it did not provide enough detailed guidance to prevent incorrect conclusions." It also concluded that there had not been a sufficient number of back-up reviews to catch any incorrect conclusions. Actions were assigned to revise the procedure governing the process and add additional reviews of the final product. No mention was made of the fact that the engineer had simply made a mistake. He had read one of his technical charts incorrectly. Adding additional reviews is a common but not very efficient or effective corrective action for errors. It is not unlike concluding that if having a highly qualified jockey on a race horse is a good thing, then having two highly qualified jockeys on the horse will be better.

Other important aspects to look for in reading evaluative information are the most commonly found weaknesses described below:

1. **Poorly based conclusions**
    A typical example of this is the conclusion that training is good because performance is good. That's like telling a person who just ate two Whoppers and a double cheese pizza that he eats properly because his current weight is about right for his height. It does not recognize the time delay between cause and effect of activities such as training. Any conclusion should have a clear and credible basis.

2. **Lack of perspective**
    This is usually evident in use of the words "not always." Such words are often used, but really serve as a red flag warning that the describer is likely hesitant to describe a problem in a critical fashion

that would make it clear but might raise the ire of the receiver of the information. For example, a report I once reviewed stated, as a problem, that "Attendance at continuing training has not always attained management's expectations." What does that mean? Does it mean that one student, one time, didn't go to training? Does it mean that most people don't go to training most of the time? It could mean anything along the spectrum bounded by these two statements. Regarding this point, here is a guide to remember: Nothing "always" does anything. Use of the "not always" term is usually symptomatic of trying to downplay issues. It allows admitting there is a problem just in case someone else finds it, while at the same time applying sufficient cosmetics to its description such that if someone else does not find it, the organization hasn't admitted how ugly its baby really is. If management down plays problems, don't waste your time trying to find workers who will object to this reduction in pressure on them, especially if the workers had a hand in causing the problems in the first place.

3. **Evidence of a lack of individual accountability**
    Some individual should be accountable for the state or condition of every physical thing in an organization, be it a piece of equipment, an area or room, a procedure, or a program defined by a procedure. It should be relatively easy to identify that person for any state of any item. A boss I once worked for insisted that for any and every problem that was reported to him (and he wanted all problems reported to him), he wanted to first be able to physically touch the person who would accept full responsibility for that problem (without pointing to others) and have that person explain

why it occurred and what was being done to correct it. Practicing this technique if one is a manager, or applying it to assess the degree of individual accountability if one is an observer, is a useful way to get insight into problems. If this individual accountability isn't readily apparent, it likely isn't there. An example of a lack of clear and strong accountability is this statement, which came out of another report I once reviewed: "Several problems occurred because management systems do not set and reinforce standards." Who would you go to see in order to get this problem fixed? Where does this "management systems" sit and to whom does he report? Remember that systems, procedures, and other inanimate objects don't cause problems. Just as problems can only be caused by people, not things, so can problems only be corrected by people, not things.

INDICATORS

Indicators or metrics are commonly recognized as good for managers to use. Their goodness is the seed grown into the often referred to adage, "If you want to improve it, measure it." Unfortunately, they're not that good, and it is not that unusual to find an over reliance on indicators at the root of some organizational ignorance.

Indicators also provide the observer valuable insight into the management of an organization, but not the way in which most people would think. Indicators, because of the shortfalls they might have, are among those fruitful places to get insights into how a place is really managed.

First of all, be aware that, regardless of what people may call them,

26. ALL INDICATORS ARE NOT "PERFORMANCE" INDICATORS

The term "performance indicator" can be misleading. There are few real indicators of performance. Most indicators are measures of process or activities. This is a significant point, for a reason to be explained shortly.

Over-zealous application of the axiom that, if you want to improve it, measure it, is the reason for thick volumes of uncountable numbers of indicators lying on shelves, unmonitored, their loneliness a result of their own massive volume. If you want to check for this malady in an organization, sit with a manager and ask him to explain what each indicator that he receives data on means and why he measures it. Be ready for long periods of silence.

Take an example that is hypothetical, but accurately describes the above downside attribute of indicators. With minor changes the example can likely be made to fit the indicators used in your organization: A firm, let's call it Efficient-widget, manufactures widgets. Let's say these are cylindrical widgets that are cut from square blocks that are stamped out of an amorphous mass of widget material.

For this example we'll measure the number of kilo-widgets produced, and call this "P". Stamping and cutting steps each take time, so we'll measure those, as "Ts" (for time to stamp), and "Tc" (for time to cut). Of these three indicators, P is the performance indicator, and Tc and Ts are the process indicators. Why? The answer is because, if Ts and Tc are indicating well, but P is not, Efficient-widget will soon be out of business. Is P the only performance indicator one would need in order to monitor performance of the company? Hardly. The cutting tool is sharp and the persons doing the cutting may continually need to be replaced while they undergo medical treatment for cuts on a variety of body parts. So another indicator might be the number of industrial safety incidents (or body cuts). Let's call this "I". If I is large, performance of Efficient-widget is not good. (All the money from production may be going into medical care, or lawsuits!) So, I is a performance indicator. Now the conscientious manager may want to monitor the number of times the people doing the cutting are found not wearing protective gloves. Call this "Ng" (for no gloves). If Ng is large, but P is large, and I is small, Efficient-widget is performing well. Therefore Ng, although it may be a valuable indicator, is a process rather than a performance indicator. The observation-related problem involving this principle occurs when the observer, be she an oversight person, the CEO, or even a board member, receives an indicator report that, if given only a cursory review, sends a highly positive and misleading message. Eighteen out of twenty indicators are doing exceptionally well. They are in the green zone. Yet the only two that are not in the green zone, P and I, indicate we are not producing anything and we're cutting the hell out of ourselves.

This example can be continued on, but enough should be here to demonstrate the principle, which is simple but important and often overlooked or not understood. Don't be misled by an indicator summary that looks great, if the inputs are primarily process indicators. You may be looking at a great set of numbers for a company that is going down the tubes. This has happened on more than one occasion.

27. USE PERFORMANCE INDICATORS TO JUDGE PERFORMANCE AND PROCESS INDICATORS TO DIAGNOSE PROBLEMS

Cut to the chase when needing to get a quick impression of an organization's performance, and skip the process indicator observation until you are ready to delve more thoroughly into problem causes.

An even more important principle regarding indicators is,

28. PERFORMANCE INDICATORS DON'T TELL THE WHOLE STORY

It would be great if they did. This would provide that magic instrument that so many senior executives are looking for -- an instrument that allows them to sit in their offices and watch it, and thereby know what's going on, without ever having to go out into the workplace and get hot, or dirty, or challenged by the workers, or made otherwise uncomfortable.

For one thing, it is not unusual for indicators to be inaccurate, or misleading -- sometimes on purpose. I recall one facility that was receiving accolades for reducing the number of improper electrical connections in a production facility such that there was a continuously declining trend of these, that is, until it was discovered that they were being reduced by calling them something different from what they were originally tracked as, and then no longer counting them.

At another facility, overdue tasks had been eliminated so quickly it raised my suspicion. Some follow-up uncovered that simultaneous with the reduction in the some 500 overdue tasks, 200 tasks appeared in a new task tracking system. The latter were now treated as being in a newly defined state of "suspended." Also, 300 other tasks had been newly defined as "deferred." The net change, or degree of improvement, after wading through the renaming, was zero!

Indicators by themselves give less than half the picture of performance of an organization. Those organizations that don't understand this will at one time or another be misled by numbers. Do you want to drive down the number of defective widgets? No problem. Send the message to Joe, to stop identifying defective widgets. Few managers would knowingly send this message, but I have seen an uncountable number of examples of managers sending such a message unintentionally. Do you want to have the pay of the company's boss based on the number of widgets he produces? No problem -- unless the boss is pushed hard enough and not watched closely enough that he starts cutting corners, which in turn puts the company at risk with either the public or some regulator, or causes some other longer term problem that won't be evident for several years.

It seems that the more an organization is "under the gun" to improve performance, the more likely that organization is to, purposely or otherwise, manipulate its indicators. The problem of indicator manipulation has been found to be so consistently a problem in troubled organizations that a colleague of mine once coined the axiom:

29. *BAD ORGANIZATIONS CAN'T COUNT*

My personal experiences and challenges of this have found it to be a statement that can be taken to the bank.

Other common problems with indicators and the reports they come in include,

1. **Information overload**
    Such overload often results in the report not being understood by management. Managers are typically smart people, but many indicator reports have so much superfluous information that it's unrealistic to expect an already overtaxed manager to take

the time to read it all. Consequently, the valuable information that is in the report is masked by the volume.

2.   **Overly subjective progress reports**
Progress is commented on only in general terms, or without basis, with statements such as, "Progress was made in all areas" -- a generally euphoric message, usually designed to keep the boss from asking hard questions.

3.   **A preponderance of gray information**
When informational content is primarily in the middle of the information spectrum or in the gray area, this often indicates an attempt to avoid the real issues. It could also be a sign of ignorance. I have seen executive summaries that are nothing more than a long list of everything that was done in the last quarter, including the most mundane activities, described by statements such as, "A meeting was held to discuss concepts ..." The latter statement is not a status of results, it's a deflective shield designed to hide or at least fog the results or lack of them.

Indicators, even if accurate and honest, are a measure of what happened in the past, not what is happening today, or what will happen tomorrow. Some will argue that "leading" indicators can be developed and these will tell the future. Forget it. If you ever come up with a reliable means of telling the future, quit your job and get into gambling or investing (some may argue these are the same). You'll be a millionaire in short order.

If you want the full and most accurate picture of an organization, indicators are useful, but they need to be augmented with considerable additional knowledge, most importantly that of the performance of individuals. You've got to get out and see what the workers are doing. You've got to observe.

TALKING (and LISTENING)

In the course of conversing with people, unless you're not interested in being efficient, remember to,

30. *ASK EVALUATIVE RATHER THAN INFORMATIVE QUESTIONS*

Again, this is a corollary to the principle of differentiating between Black, White, and Gray information. Informative questions are those such as, how does this process work? Or, what is the structure of the organization? This kind of information can and should be gleaned during advance preparations, using the wide array of documents readily available in most organizations. To ask a working person to tell you what some procedure says is not only inefficient use of the time of both the observer and the observee, it is also an insult to the organization being observed. The question implies that your time is so much more valuable than theirs that you choose to not do your homework and read the material but rather prefer that they read it and tell you what it says. (Note the special case in which you are quizzing a person to determine if she knows what the procedure says. This is obviously not a question asked for general information.)

Evaluative questions are those questions that allow you to discern between one degree of quality and another, to draw a conclusion or make a judgment, or to evaluate something. These questions might include asking a manager what the state of cleanliness of some area is, when you have already looked at that area and made a judgment on its cleanliness yourself.

The question then allows you to make a judgment of the manager's knowledge of the state (and, therefore, indirectly, the frequency of his presence in the work place), or perhaps of his standards for cleanliness. Other questions allowing judgment to be made include, What are you doing about the problem? (The judgment would be based on a comparison of the response with what you believe are the best actions to be taken to address the problem.) How do you know what those in the workplace are really doing? (Again, the judgment would be based on the observer's experienced-based opinion of how the interviewee should be keeping apprised of how his direct reports are performing in the workplace.) It takes effort and considerable advance preparation to develop evaluative questions. This is precisely why some observers don't ask them, except for happenstance.

In addition to a series of evaluative questions prepared in advance, a good observer will also have the following series of questions at the ready. These can provide considerable insight into any observed problem:

31. *WHY IS THE PROBLEM OCCURRING? WHY DIDN'T SELF-ASSESSMENT IDENTIFY IT? WHO'S ACCOUNTABLE FOR FIXING IT? WHAT'S BEING DONE ABOUT IT? AND HOW WILL YOU KNOW WHEN IT'S FIXED?*

If you're talking to a responsible person and there is not a clear and concise answer to each and every one of these, you are likely looking at the problem.

There are several proven techniques that will help the observer to,

32. *GET THE MOST OUT OF EVERY INTERVIEW*

1. **Be prepared.** Never, ever go into an interview

unprepared. You will waste your time as well as that of the person to whom you are talking. Go through the exercise first, of defining for yourself what you want to get out of the interview. What is your objective in conducting the interview? This may be something as simple as determining if the manager understands what is happening in his area; or it may be slightly more complex, and have several aspects, such as to determine if there is alignment between this person and other levels of management; how effective is the vertical communications chain; what do the workers see as their responsibility for resolving problems. The 3X5 card approach discussed in AACT 17 [USE 3X5 CARDS] is indispensable in this regard.

2.   **Set the interviewee(s) at ease.** This is a good time to apply the principle that when all else fails, try telling the truth. My practice is to always assume all else will fail, and go right to the truth. It really works! Tell those being interviewed the reason for your assessment. Assure them you are not interested in individuals, and assure them nothing they say will be attributed to the specific individual saying it (If this is true, and hopefully it is). The amount of detail and personal reassurances that need to be given in these circumstances vary depending on the experiences and maturity of the interviewees. Working level personnel who perceive they have been "done wrong" by management before may need more assurance than senior level executives. (On the other hand, some executives, lacking the natural innocence of the workers, may need even more assurance.)

3.   **Let the interviewee know that she is free to look**

at your notes at any time, and then be prepared to allow her to do so. If the note taking is done in a professional way, as it should be in all cases, this will not pose a problem, and will assure the interviewee that you are interested in accuracy in your notes and not targeting her specifically to report on to her boss.

4.   **Use group interviews.** These work particularly well with front-line personnel and their supervisors who tend to feel more threatened in an individual interview. The group atmosphere takes some of the tension out of the interaction, and can get people talking and building on points made by others in the group. Often times, the only time you can get some workers together is during lunch time. This is even better. Don't be cheap. Buy them lunch. Nothing breaks down inhibitions and barriers as well as a few shared pizzas. As mentioned earlier, a pizza is one my most valuable assessment tools.

5.   **Differentiate between those who <u>want</u> to do something and those who actually do it.** Essentially everyone <u>wants </u>to do good, so accept this up front. Acceptance of this will move all of the best intentions of everyone you talk to into the area of gray info, where they can quickly be disregarded as far as being of any assessment value. Continually drive on what that person is actually and personally <u>doing</u> to effect positive change.

6.   **Remember that it takes more than managers to run an operation.** Consequently, it is important to bring the actions (or inactions) of the workers into the discussion. Talk to the workers. Find out if they are aligned. Alignment between the managers

and these workers is essential. If there is not close alignment between what the manager sees as the problems and what the workers see as the problems, and if the workers are not doing something <u>specific</u> to fix the problems, then what would ever cause the problems to get fixed? I have found this gap between management and the workforce so frequently that I consider it to be a common occurrence. I recall many organizations in which managers told me they had major efforts underway to improve performance. Signs, banners, and newsletter articles heralded the improvement initiatives. But when I asked the front-line workers what they, as individuals, were doing to improve their performance, or what they were doing differently as a result of the initiative, I got little more than blank stares in response.

7.   **Avoid general questions**. These leave too much room for the person you are having the discussion with to, advertently or inadvertently, absorb all of the interview time. In some cases the response will consist of dancing around the issues and, in most cases, it will include spewing gray information that will waste your time as well as his. For example, instead of asking, "How effective are corrective actions in this organization?" do your homework in advance and (if this is true) have at least several examples of where corrective action was not effective. Then put a point on the question more like: You have had this repeat problem, indicating that whatever corrective action you took was not effective. Why, in your opinion, was it not effective?

8.   **Ask the workers what the problems are**. Those in the workplace on a regular basis typically know what the organization's problems are. They certainly

know what problems they have to deal with on a regular basis and are more than happy to talk about them to anyone who will listen. These questions can be direct, such as: What do you see as the biggest problem in this organization related to safety (or production or whatever you happen to be looking into). Or the softer, open-ended version: If you were King (or Queen) for the day, and could change one thing to improve safety in this organization, what would that be? The insight of the workforce is invaluable in determining where and how an organization needs to improve. Unfortunately, it's a source that, strangely enough, is a well from which many managers rarely drink.

9.   **Insist that people discuss problem areas**. If you are conducting an observation with the goal of helping an organization to improve its performance, then don't waste your time and that of others by dwelling on what is good in the organization. I was once physically threatened by an executive because I doggedly refused to spend any of my very limited time touring a new training facility that was under construction. I had been tasked by the CEO of this organization with providing my overall impression of the operation of one of his complex technical facilities, and doing this after a total visit time of only four hours. Being interested in getting right into the issues, rather than taking the tour, which would provide no evaluative information, I insisted instead on discussing the poor condition of the current training facility and how it got that way. I was interested in what would be done differently to maintain the condition of the new facility and prevent it from quickly degrading to the condition of the current facility. (Polite but tenacious is the

guideline to follow in such situations.) Based on my impressions following this discussion (that he eventually relented to), much needed to be done to change the behaviors of those who would use the new facility. Otherwise it would soon be in the same state as the old facility. Considering the gaping holes in the executive's attention that this discussion laid bare, had I been him I also would have preferred walking around and bragging about the new facility.

10. **Look for results not effort.** I was once told by a manager to whom I had just delivered the unfortunate conclusion that his company was slipping behind his competitors in fundamental performance: "Our performance has not declined, it's just that everyone else has gotten much better." This is like having the jockey in a race on which you just bet your life savings tell you, "We aren't winning, but that's not so bad because we're running a lot faster than we've run before." As another example, I was once apprised at great length of all of the "deliverables" that had been produced as a result of an action plan to improve the productivity rate in an organization. Essentially all of the deliverables reflected effort rather than results, and included such items as, "developed a new procedure governing the production process," and "developed a new and thorough set of indicators." Unfortunately for the facility, the production rate was unchanged.

11. **Remember that talk is cheap.** Most savvy managers know the right answers to questions asked by observers, but their words sometimes don't match reality. Asking them to give concrete examples is one way of cutting through any public relations

pitches and collecting objective information that allows a meaningful judgment to be made. Valueless comments I often have heard managers respond with when asked a question intended to gauge their understanding of their organization's performance, include, "We can always do better. No one is perfect." Who could argue with this statement? But what does it say of their understanding of the real status? These same managers are usually unable to articulate what their organization's problems are, either because they think they don't have problems, or they are unaware of what their problems are. Similarly, in response to an inquiry about a problem, the existence of which is obvious, managers often talk at great length about how the problem is "unacceptable," or how "outraged" they are about the problem. But again, so what? The real question is what are they <u>doing</u> about the problem -- <u>specifically</u> what are they doing and can they provide any examples?

12. **Be skeptical.** If someone tells you he did something (to fix an important problem, for example), be Reaganesque and apply AACT 16 [GO SEE FOR YOURSELF]. Determine if he really did it. Again, managers don't often lie, but sometimes their hopes overwhelm reality. If a senior manager tells you she has made her expectations clear to her people, track down a few of her people and ask them what the manager's expectations are. You may be surprised at what you find.

13. **Have empathy, not sympathy.** Empathy is an appreciation for the difficulty of solving problems; it is an understanding of the challenges that come with the tough jobs; it is what comes from having

walked a mile in another person's wingtips (or heels). Sympathy goes a step further and sets the groundwork for accepting that the problem is too hard to solve, or that life is so tough for this person that you begin to make excuses for him. Be particularly alert for people trying to tell you how hard the job is, or what all the barriers are to getting something done. Barriers are what people see when they're not focused on the final goal. When a response is centered around a description of how hard a job is, I maintain my politeness to the person, but position my line of questioning with the mindset: "OK, let's all agree up front that life is hard. Now let's put that behind us and get on to more meaningful discussions of what the problem is and what you're doing about it."

14. **Focus on the empty half of the glass.** If you do otherwise you'll never identify what's needed to fill it. I recall one organization that had just received an independent assessment of its training programs. The report indicated the programs were better than they had ever been. The managers were ecstatic. When I asked what they had learned from the review, they said there had been only one adverse comment, and that it was a "data-base nit." In reality, the comment was that there were several data bases, into which important action items had been entered and then never tracked or closed out; consequently, some of the worker's qualifications were no longer valid. Some other comments in the report also said the assessment team was doubtful this organization could complete what they needed to by the time they were required to complete it. This would have been a great heads up to senior management had his middle managers not obscured the point by

telling him about the stuff that made the glass half full.

In summary of the above, in interviews,

33. BE SKEPTICAL, GET TO THE POINT, LOOK FOR RESULTS, AND EXPECT THE HIGHEST STANDARDS IN EVERYTHING

WATCHING

Observation space can be divided into three realms: people, places, and documents. All of these can be observed, but people are clearly the most important to observe.

34. IF YOU WANT TO UNDERSTAND WHAT'S GOING ON IN AN ORGANIZATION, WATCH THE PEOPLE. CONVERSELY, IF YOU DON'T WATCH THE PEOPLE, YOU WON'T KNOW WHAT'S REALLY GOING ON IN AN ORGANIZATION

Observations of places and documents provide value only because they are symptomatic of what people do -- or don't do. The bottom line is, for the greatest assessment value, observe the people. Observe them doing their jobs. I once visited a technical facility that had been known across the nation as one of the top performing organizations in the country. This reputation was slowly fading and had been fading over the course of about two years. Upon my arrival at the facility, at the risk of being discourteous, I skipped the usual introductory discussions with the senior managers and went right out into the workplace. A summary of the "black" information from my notes follows:

1.   When the technical workers communicated with each other regarding the highly complex

equipment they were operating, rather than closing the communication loop in a way that ensures the message or direction was clearly heard and understood, they often used the more cursory response, "OK."

2. It was not unusual to see supervisors performing tasks that workers should have been performing, rather than having workers perform the task while the supervisors provided the supervision and oversight.

3. In a training simulator, the personnel in training rarely referred to alarm response procedures whenever an alarm annunciated, instead carrying out their actions from memory and occasionally leaving out a step or two.

4. Classroom instructors generally did not ensure that the students were mentally engaged in the training activity by asking questions and involving the students. They were also less than careful about ensuring their overheads and other training aides could be clearly seen by all in the class.

5. Workers in the facility were not particularly careful to ensure they did not spread industrial waste outside of work areas that were supposedly controlled so that this spread did not occur. I saw at least four examples of this in about a half-hour.

6. Several workers who were engaged in work on electrically energized equipment were wearing neck chains; one wore an earring. The jewelry, although quite stylish, presented the very real possibility of exacerbating the burns that would result should an

inadvertent contact with the energized equipment occur.

7. A technician working inside of an electrical switchboard inserted his pen as a temporary pin to prevent an electrical relay from actuating during his work. A very clever approach, but one that increased the likelihood of the pen slipping out, causing the relay to actuate and cause a substantial amount of equipment damage -- certainly a greater likelihood than if the proper tool had been used.

People get paid to do a job. They get paid to do it right, and "right" includes doing it safely. Every one of the above observations is a case of someone not doing his job. The question I was interested in was, Why? In pulling the string, I made several additional observations, which included these:

8. I looked at records to determine what kind of incidents or errors were occurring at this facility, and found, as I suspected I would, one significant event and several other noteworthy events that had been caused by personnel errors.

9. In response to a question on why a supervisor did not react to one of his people doing something improperly, the supervisor candidly admitted he was "uncomfortable confronting people."

10. Several supervisors of the workers who were confirming receipt of complex communications with "OK" were aware of the concept of closed loop communications (in which both the sender and the receiver verify the communicated message has been

properly sent and received) but "just hadn't thought about it." In fact, I observed them complementing the workers on their overall good performance, specifically mentioning the "generally good communications."

11. Again, in pulling the string, I found that training guidance provided very clear expectations for instructors to engage students in classroom training activities. The guidance also included specifics on how to do this.

12. The organization's safety manual clearly said that jewelry on workers engaged in electrical work was verboten.

Based on my follow-up observations, I formulated the following conclusions. Items considered to be bases for the conclusions are indicated by the item numbers in parentheses.

A. Workers are not performing to the standards expected by management. (1-7, 11, 12)

B. The above behaviors are contributing to problems. (8)

C. The supervisors not setting or reinforcing expectations is a key contributor to this substandard performance. (2,9,10)

These conclusions turned out to be exactly why the organization's performance was slipping. Over time, some of the more experienced supervisors had been replaced with new, less experienced people. These new supervisors were somewhat intimidated by the highly experienced workers and tended to not confront, and in some cases, even to avoid contact with the workers. A large gap had developed in the communication chain between the managers who were expecting one thing and the workers who were doing something else. This gap, as it usually does, occurred at the supervisor level. The workforce over time developed the habit of doing what each individual felt like doing and received no coaching in the course of it.

The only way to determine if the above malady, which is not an unusual one, is occurring in any organization is to observe the people doing their jobs.

NEVER GO OUT ALONE

35. *TOUR GUIDES PROVIDE AN ADDED OPPORTUNITY*

A person with the right experience can walk through almost any facility alone and identify a number of problems. However, this would not be the best use of his time, because this lone ranger would be working at about 50 % efficiency, leaving at least half of the most useful information on the table. For example, if he sees that the floor is dirty, or that equipment is poorly stored and likely to get damaged, this might be a useful observation. But wouldn't it be more useful to also see whether or not one of the facility's managers identified the same things, and if not, why not? And when these items are discussed with that manager, wouldn't it be useful to get his views on why the conditions exist? What will it take to not only fix them but to prevent their recurrence? This additional information is the stuff of insight.

In the course of looking at things, it is generally most useful for the observer, be he from an outside organization, or from within the organization, to get a "tour guide" to go with him around the facility. It is most helpful if the guide is also someone responsible for the areas toured. The guide's actions and reactions to things seen will tell you more about the organization than the things themselves. Pay special attention to items such as the following: Is it apparent that he (the tour guide) gets in the work area frequently? Do people know him and say hello to him? Does he know how to access remote parts of the facility? Is he familiar with the procedures to get into any controlled areas? How familiar is he with facility processes and people? How familiar is he with and how well does he adhere to facility policies? How does he react when he sees a problem?

MEETINGS

36. *AS MEETINGS GO, SO GOES THE ORGANIZATION*

Meetings are another place where managers often ply their trade. Unfortunately, for some, this is the place they ply their trade for the majority of their work time. Consequently, meetings provide an opportunity to gaze into the world of the manager and acquire meaningful insight for any assessment.

Things to look for in observing a meeting include:

1. **Is someone in charge?**
   Are the managers using this forum to set clear expectations, or do they essentially beg and cajole when they try to get something from the attendees? Look for every opportunity to set or reinforce expectations, and if the managers do not take advantage of each of these opportunities, make note of it. Follow-up will be needed, but you can feel confident that if expectations are not being set or

reinforced in meetings, they are probably similarly so out in the workplace.

2.   Is there a sense of discipline to the meeting?
It should start and finish on time, and should move through the agenda crisply(certainly there should be an agenda). If such is not the case, take note of how many people are in the meeting. A quick calculation will result in a compelling statement on the amount of manpower (and expended salary) that is wasted. Conducting a meeting "on schedule" is the mark of a top notch organization. This is not only apparent in the performance of many companies, but is also a carry over from my experience in the submarine force. When a well run submarine was to leave port at 4:00 PM (or 1600), you could set your watch when the last line was cast off. It would leave the bollard on the pier at precisely 4:00 PM. Similarly, when a sub had managed to build a less than stellar reputation for performance, and there were not many of these, their operations overall would be sloppy. Schedule meant little to them and this would show in the timeliness of their activities.

3.   Is there a results focus to the meeting?
Discussions should continually drive to what was achieved, what was accomplished, what were the results. Metrics should be used to include objectivity in status reports, and accountability for results should be evident.

4.   **Is the discussion primarily "happy talk"?**
Happy talk and what it is reflective of is a concept that will be discussed further when we get to AACT 61. For now, accept that this is the kind of discussion that is enjoyable (albeit not useful) to engage in.

Pleasantries are frequently exchanged. Whatever is going well is dwelled upon. Compliments flow freely, but problem areas are essentially never discussed -- and consequently not dealt with. I recall one meeting in which the Safety Supervisor took the opportunity to congratulate everyone on what he said was "excellent" performance by the night shift in responding to a problem that had occurred during an evolution the previous night. He also mentioned that following the recovery, the evolution would be conducted again on the day shift. My critical mind wondered why the problem had occurred in the first place. Applying AACT 15 [PULL THE STRING] I observed the second performance of the evolution and talked to those involved. The reality of the situation was that people did respond very well to the previous night's problem, but the problem had occurred because a number of safety rules and company policies had been violated: The evolution started before it should have because there was no coordination between the several work groups involved, and no supervision or management was present during the evolution to provide guidance when things started to go off track. Even more interesting, these same shortfalls were evident in the second performance of this evolution, and it was only because of blind luck that the same problem did not recur.

5. **Do room conditions reflect high standards?**
    Remember that whenever the boss is present when performance or conditions are substandard and the boss does not question them, she de facto sends the message to all present that this performance or condition is acceptable. Consequently, meeting rooms are one of those places where it is useful to

pay attention to the conditions. A long time ago I saw the correlation between the conditions that are accepted in a facility and the capability of the management. This correlation holds true, not only for rooms containing working equipment, but also meeting rooms. I recall one corporate organization where in a meeting with the CEO, I couldn't help be distracted by the condition of the Board Room. It was dirty! The Board Room was dirty! The trash cans were overflowing. Whoever had used it previously had left soft-drink cans on the beautiful mahogany table. Even the cover of the light switch was on loose, crooked, and held on with only one of the two mounting screws. Within a couple of years after this meeting, the CEO and all of the executive managers of this organization had been replaced. Although the management purge was not directly related to the Board Room conditions, those conditions were symptomatic of the fact that management had relaxed to the point that they began to routinely accept low standards. This eventually became apparent in the operation of their facilities. Think about this when you see substandard conditions that are accepted in any scenario.

CHAPTER 5
OBSERVING THE PERIMETER

There are a number of elements in any organization that function on the perimeter of the main business vortex. These are the support organizations or functions that are performed not to directly provide the product or service of a facility but rather to support the safe and efficient provision of those products and services. A look into the effectiveness of these peripheral elements can provide considerable insight into how well an organization is managed and operating, and thus insight on how that organization can improve its performance. These functions, therefore, warrant comprehensive observation.

TRAINING

An entire book could be written on assessing or observing the training function, but the most fundamental principle to be remembered in observing this area is,

37. *TRAINING IS A MICROCOSM OF AN ORGANIZATION*

Whatever is happening in the conduct of training, be it good or bad, is likely to also be happening in the conduct of main line operations. The quality of performance in training will mirror the quality of performance in main line operations. The amount and effectiveness of oversight of training will not be unlike the amount and effectiveness of oversight of main line operations.

Thus a look at training is a look at the entire organization, and observation of training aspects such as the following will provide an excellent view of how well an organization is operating overall:

1.   **The conditions of the training area**
      Look closely and critically at the conditions in the training facility -- the cleanliness, the orderliness, the adherence to posted directions, the dress and attitudes of the Training staff, and how current and accurate the training materials are. Recognize that the standards reflected by these conditions are the first standards to which new employees will be exposed. These are the silent directions to the employees that say, "This is what we expect of you." What you see when you look at these aspects will describe generally how the organization is run, whether or not the trainers operate to high standards and follow their own procedures and policies, and to what degree the organization values training and, therefore, the development and skills of their workforce. If employees in training are not treated as the valuable resource they are, there is little reason to think they will be treated any differently in the workplace.

2.   **The integration of training**

Look for integration of the Training staff's efforts with those of line   management. This will indicate whether or not training is considered to be an important element of the organization. I recall one facility where performance problems indicated a major weakness in the knowledge and skills of the workforce, with a direct link to the poor quality of the training program. This organization was subsequently required by a regulatory agency to do a self-analysis of the substandard performance and to specifically determine why line management was not more involved in and supportive of the training programs, and why Training and line personnel seemed to be working in separate silos. Guess who facility management assigned to do the analysis -- the Training staff! And with neither input from nor involvement of line management! Following the analysis, a plan was developed to recover the quality of the training program. Eighty-eight of the 93 planned actions were assigned -- to the Training organization! You shouldn't be surprised when I tell you this particular Improvement effort didn't work.

3.   **The value placed on training insight**

Look for the "presence" of the Training Manager at key plant meetings. Presence includes more than attendance. It includes meaningful participation and interaction in the meeting. Training manager presence will indicate whether or not this position is considered to be that of a valuable member of the management team. It will also indicate if and how insights of someone with training expertise are considered in key decisions, as they should be.

4.   **The value placed on training**
There is one fundamental question that can
be asked to quickly determine whether or not
management places value on training: Is training
useful in achieving the bottom line, i.e. is it used
to improve performance? If training is truly used
to improve performance, then the market will drive
the line managers to use training more because of
the value it adds. On the other hand, if training
is done primarily because it's required by law or
regulation, or just so that one can say the training
was done, then the training adds little if any value
and becomes one more item on the plates of the
likely already overloaded staff. If training is used to
improve performance, it should be relatively easy to
find multiple examples of problems that no longer
exist following training targeted at those problems.

5.   **The approach to training problems**
Training problems should be dealt with just as
rigorously as any other problems. Consequently, just
as with any problem at a facility, management should
be able to clearly articulate a response to AACT 31
[WHY IS THE PROBLEM OCCURRING? WHY
DIDN'T SELF-ASSESSMENT IDENTIFY IT? WHO
IS ACCOUNTABLE FOR FIXING IT? WHAT'S
BEING DONE ABOUT IT? AND, HOW WILL YOU
KNOW WHEN IT'S FIXED?]

Little if anything is more important to the success of an
organization than having quality training. This conclusion is
founded in the value of training I came to appreciate in the
nuclear submarine force but has been reinforced time and
again by my witnessing numerous instances of training quality
swirling down the drain at organizations, only to have overall
performance follow suit some time later. These performance

declines usually resulted from management weaknesses that were first indicated by poor quality of training and then subsequently reflected in the overall management of the organization. A look at training is like a look into a crystal ball regarding the future of an organization. More on this subject follows when we get to AACT 39.

Training is like many things in life. Just because there is a lot of it doesn't mean it's good. Observation of an organization should include looking at how much and what type of training is provided, keeping in mind the point that,

38. ORGANIZATIONS OFTEN DO TOO MUCH TRAINING -- AND ON THE WRONG THINGS

This can be primarily attributed to two reasons:

1. **Training is used as "currency."**
    If you want to save yourself a lot of money, the amount of which is dependent on several factors including how big your organization is, take a look at how the "currency" of training is used. You likely will find that we sent Joe to some external course or seminar because Joe is a good guy; he's been doing a great job. Training is used as a form of compensation for Joe, rather than a tool to improve Joe's performance. The sad point of this being that the resources used to give Joe the reward are taken out of the training purse, so some needed training will go unfunded.

    To observe for the above malady, ask to see a list of the training, and particularly external training that people have attended in the last six months. Ask for or determine for yourself how much the training really cost. Many organizations will track the cost of training but do so inaccurately. The real cost of training includes not only the cost of the training and any related expense, such as travel or lodging, but also the hourly wage or portion of salary paid to the attendees while at training. Believe me, when the cost of training is tallied and clearly indicated to show this wage portion of the expense, it will call a lot of attention to the application of training. I once ran a large corporate training organization in which I insisted for a period of time that any requests to send individuals to training outside of the company clearly indicate at the top of the request form, the estimated cost of the training, with the calculation of the cost to include the number of individuals going to the training and the total of their salary cost that would be expended while they were at the training. Some of the resulting numbers turned out to be so high that the requestors were too embarrassed to submit the requests.

It is also useful for the observer of training to select a few training activities and determine who approved each training activity. Then find the Approver and ask what the <u>basis</u> was for approving the training. If the answer is other than to correct or prevent a specific problem, it likely indicates use of the training currency.

And finally, the training observer will want to find some evidence of completed training that was reported as having been "valuable." Be aware that any training doled out as "currency" is usually appreciated and rarely criticized for fear the donation may not be made again in the future. Ask if what was reported as valuable training was subsequently brought in house so that the next time someone needs the same training, it will not have to be repurchased at a repeat of the same cost.

2.   **Much "required" training owes its longevity to myths.**
In the real world, only a certain amount of time can be allotted to training. Many fields of expertise, particularly in high hazard industries, have a certain amount of training that is required by law to be conducted. If one works through the exercise of defining exactly what the basis is for the content and frequency of "required" training, it will not be unusual to find that the training being conducted is considerably more extensive than that actually required by the law or regulation. This inflated amount of training is maintained because of a misguided belief by management that it is indeed required. Much of this excessive and unnecessary training is a result of the "kingdoms" that often get established when highly motivated people are assigned to lead a training effort without sufficient guidance, direction, or oversight. Mary is responsible for Emergency Response training. So Mary, in an effort to make this the best Emergency Response training in the country or maybe even the world, and without an appreciation of the bigger picture, adds to and refines the training until it is the Cadillac of all Emergency Response training programs on earth. The problem is this unnecessary training ties up resources that would be better applied to training that is truly needs-based. A detailed inquiry into the basis of "required" training can uncover this squandered expense.

The above kind of critical probing during an observation of training can save a customer company a remarkable amount of employee time and company money. I once conducted this exercise at a large corporation and ended up with a net annual savings of close to a million dollars. More importantly, the savings achieved are resources that can be applied to truly improve performance.

LOOKING INTO THE FUTURE

There are often precursors to organizational problems. Unfortunately these are easier to see after the fact rather than at a time that would allow them to be useful in predicting problems before they occur. Such is not the case with Training.

39. TRAINING PROBLEMS FORESHADOW ORGANIZATIONAL PROBLEMS

Except in the rarest of cases, if the performance of an organization is good, it is good because the people are good. The people are good in large measure because they know what they are doing, and this in turn can be attributed to good training. But if the training at one of these "good" organizations turns suddenly poor, or is stopped, the performance will not immediately follow suit. It will take some time before the knowledge and skills of the employees fade, and thus the performance of the organization suffers. It is this time delay which makes training one of the most valuable areas to observe. As stated earlier, looking at training is like looking into a crystal ball. By virtue of the fact that training problems precede organizational performance problems, precursors of training problems are true precursors of organizational problems. Years of experience have shown that if any of the following exist in Training, they are harbingers of significant problems coming, both in training and subsequently in the performance of the organization. These are,

1. Lack of line ownership of training
2. Weak self-assessments of training
3. Student dissatisfaction

Anyone observing the area of Training would be remiss to not include these three items in the scope of their observations.

CORPORATE SUPPORT, PRINCIPLES, AND LINE OWNERSHIP OF TRAINING

It is useful in multi-site organizations interested in providing efficient as well as effective training, to have strong corporate oversight of training. Appendix 1 is a set of specific expectations for corporate oversight of training that I developed as a vice president of training at a large corporation. An effective observer would look for clearly defined expectations and could use those in Appendix 1 as a guide with which to gauge the comprehensiveness and clarity of expectations.

It is also useful to have a set of principles when leading people in any endeavor, rather than volumes of rules and regulations. A set of training principles I have used is provided as Appendix 2. The existence or absence of these or similar principles is a good and easily used indicator of whether or not the training effort (and, as discussed above, the entire facility effort) is well managed. These also can be used by an observer as a ruler of sorts.

Much of the above is based on the proven training principle that for training to be effective, line management must "own" training; however, what "ownership" means in this regard is often misunderstood or inadequately communicated. Consequently, this important principle is often not reinforced and all suffer. Training personnel, line managers, and for the purpose of this book, observers, need to know what line management ownership of training looks like. Observable behaviors indicative of line ownership of training are provided as Appendix 3.

SELF-ASSESSMENT

Self-assessment is another of the vital support functions of any well run organization. There may be a separate element of the organization that has the primary responsibility for coordinating or overseeing self-assessment. At some facilities, the self-assessment function may be entirely executed by the line management of the facility. The third possible configuration of the self-assessment function is a combination of both those just mentioned. Regardless of the configuration, the importance of self-assessment cannot be overstated. It is the mechanism by which an organization observes itself and then makes adjustments to continually improve. Going back to the car analogy discussed at the outset of this book, the person who is accelerating, braking, and steering the car is taking these actions because she is simultaneously assessing where the car is and where it needs to go. The back seat driver is that separate function that also assesses but from a different viewpoint and encourages the driver to "slow down," or "turn here." A combination of these with any married couple, if it doesn't first result in divorce, will usually serve both parties well and get them to where they want to be, safely and efficiently. Thus self-assessment is important, and being important, it needs to be observed.

A shortfall I have often seen with observers assessing the self-assessment function is that they get so wrapped up with the mechanics of the self-assessment process that they miss the big picture on how effective self-assessment is. Instead of looking for the effectiveness of the effort, they worry instead about how frequently the self-assessments are performed as compared to other frequencies they have seen, or if and how the self-assessment results are documented. Keeping in mind AACT 1 [THINK PERFORMANCE BASED],

40. *THE PIVOTAL QUESTION REGARDING ANY SELF-ASSESSMENT EFFORT IS NOT, WHAT IS THE QUALITY OF SELF-ASSESSMENT, BUT RATHER, DO THE MANAGERS KNOW WHAT'S GOING ON*

This can best be judged by making a list of briefly stated issues identified by observation of an organization's performance, or by recent assessments performed by outside organizations. Check off those items of which management was aware at the time they were identified. If what remains on the list is not substantial, then focusing on self-assessment capability is not worth the effort. Should one decide, based on the preceding litmus test, to review a facility's self-assessment effort, one caution would be,

41. *DON'T MINE THE SELF-ASSESSMENT DATA*

Self-assessment information provides valuable insight into an organization. Observation reports by a facility's management or any form of problem self-identification are great places to look for problems other than those evident from one's personal observations. Many oversight organizations, and particularly those with limited talent, take self-identified problems from these reports, repackage them, and deliver them to management of the facility as their product. This is like "mining" the facility's information, digging through it to find jewels of information. This practice results in telling management what they already know. It adds no value, and can even have a detrimental effect overall. On a number of occasions I have witnessed organizations that once did well at self-identifying problems slide down the performance scale because they reduced their self-assessment effort in order to reduce their exposure to having observers mine their data and publish their problems for others to see. The practice of data mining should be scrupulously avoided. On the other hand, these internal assessment reports can provide valuable insights. The following are some examples of points to look for:

1.   If the preponderance of items identified in self-assessment reports deal with conditions rather than practices, something is wrong. Conditions are the <u>result</u> of practices, and to list deficient conditions while being silent on practices is a conflict in itself. What the former likely means is that the managers are reluctant to identify practices that don't meet expectations, which would necessitate confronting workers and that for some can be an unpleasant task. This syndrome of identifying only condition issues comes about when managers are held accountable for performing observations but, being unskilled at or uncomfortable with people interactions, only comment on inanimate objects that require no confrontation.

2.   If the largest percentage of self-assessments indicate there are no problems out there, something is wrong. Recall AACT 3 [THERE ARE ALWAYS PROBLEMS OUT THERE]. The string will need to be pulled to identify what is wrong, but look first for assessors who are short on the skills needed for assessment.

The AACTs of this book can be used as a gauge in analyzing their skills.

If all of the deficiencies of a particular type are identified by only one or a small group of individuals, something is wrong. This usually indicates the assessors are wearing blinders and only looking at items within their specific area of interest or expertise. For example, while reviewing a large number of self-assessment reports from one organization I noticed that anytime a deficiency was identified with the control of ionizing radiation, it was identified by the supervisor of radiation health. After pulling the string, I identified two problems with this. First, the Radiation Health supervisor was not meeting the expectation for him to identify other deficiencies as well as those within his area of responsibility. Second, essentially none of the other managers who performed self-assessments identified deficiencies in the radiation health area. This was subsequently found to be the result of the line managers lacking ownership of radiation health performance, and relegating their responsibilities to the supervisor of that area.

INDEPENDENT OVERSIGHT

A key support element of any organization is its oversight function, whatever form it may be in. These are the guys and ladies who are not members of the family but periodically sit in the back seat of the car and watch how well you are driving. Observing this oversight function, or watching the watchers, provides a wealth of valuable information for line management. So,

42. DON'T FORGET TO WATCH THE WATCHERS

Unfortunately, some oversight organizations spend a considerable amount of their time trying to justify their existence, primarily producing voluminous reports that are not often read and coercing line managers to do things that may or may not warrant the effort when considered in the total scheme of things and in the light of other priorities. Reasons for weak oversight groups are multiple, but all can be grouped into shortfalls in the three critical attributes mentioned at the outset of this book, in AACT 2 [ENERGY, EXPOSURE, AND EXPERIENCE ARE THE REQUISITES OF A GOOD OBSERVER]. A weakness that I have frequently found in oversight organizations, including the best of these, is the tendency to continually probe the same areas over and over. Looking into areas where problems have been found before is a good idea. Doing this to an extreme that limits the observation of other important areas is a good idea gone bad. I remind those who have fallen into this trap,

43. *IF YOU CONTINUE TO DIG IN THE SAME HOLE, DON'T BE SURPRISED TO FIND THE SAME DIRT*

An assessment is like a piece of plywood with a pattern of holes in it placed over a picture of an organization's performance. Each of the holes represents one of the areas observed. We place the plywood over the picture and look into each of the holes. We then mentally construct our idea of what the organization's total "picture" of performance looks like based on the sampling of holes we have chosen to look into. If we continually use the same set of holes to work as we do our observations, eventually, issues in these holes will get resolved and our perceived picture of the organization will turn more and more positive. In reality, portions of the picture not lying beneath any of the holes go unexamined -- until a problem occurs and the ugly features of the baby become self-revealing. Uneducated observers then wonder how such a problem could occur when the assessments kept coming out so positively. The case of the infamous Davis Besse nuclear power plant event, in which a pineapple size hole in the reactor went undetected for years, is an example of how this principle came into play when outside oversight organizations didn't regularly cut new holes in their plywood.

HOW TO WATCH THE WATCHERS

One might at first not see a connection between oversight groups and salt, but consider this: In pre-industrial days, most people used "common salt." This was salt that was evaporated in salt pans or evaporation pools in bays and deltas and other shallow coastal waters. It was often gritty and filled with sand, dirt, bits of shell and other impurities. It was relatively inexpensive and affordable by most people. The more pure, high quality salt came from underground deposits that only existed in a few places in the world. This had to be mined and transported and was extremely expensive. This however was the type of salt that was needed for pickling and preserving meats. Since it was so expensive one only used it on the better, higher quality cuts of meat. Thus before using the expensive salt, the user first made sure the meat was "...worth its salt."

Similar to the above, any "better, high quality" oversight group that is worth its salt will want to know the answer to the question, Is the Oversight Group adding value (commensurate with their cost, of course)? Any observer worth his salt will want to focus any observations of oversight groups on answering the same question.

The easiest way to get an answer to the above question is to find out if problems within the organization receiving the oversight are being identified internally or if the problems are self-revealing or being found by other outside organizations such as regulatory agencies. If an oversight group does not proactively pursue the answer to the above question on a regular basis, it is reasonable to raise the question of whether the right people are in the oversight group. Reviewing a sample of their reports and a short follow-up discussion with several of them will provide an answer to that question.

It is also valuable to talk to the person in charge of the in-house Oversight Group and determine if she really feels accountable for the facility's problems. She should lay awake at night worrying that some problem might exist that her staff has not already identified and provided useful insight in solving. If a problem is either self-revealing or identified by some outside group, she should feel badly about it and should be quick to conduct a thorough self-examination of her own efforts to find out why that happened. When questioned on accountability, her response should reflect a certainty that senior management will hold her accountable for any unidentified problems and that she can appreciate and readily accepts that accountability.

Another technique that can provide some interesting insights into the performance of the Oversight Group is to put together a list of issues identified either through your personal observations, or by listing issues identified by outside oversight organizations. Include items that have made themselves evident through occurrence, such as problems in industrial safety or patient falls in a healthcare facility, made evident by a number of more recent personnel injuries. Then, within the topics or areas that encompass these problems, list the issues identified by the oversight organization. Don't accept the lame excuse that "different people identify different things." The Oversight Group should feel driven to identify everything. If its members don't, they should be replaced. I once used the above technique and found that the oversight staff had not identified that a particular facility had a large number of instances in which maintenance work had to be repeated multiple times because it had been done improperly the first time. Pulling the string on that, I concluded that there were several holes in the basic work-skill knowledge of the maintenance workers. In pursuing why the above item was missed by the Oversight Group, I sensed that this particular group had a compliance mentality and would only identify those items that were clear violations of regulations. I followed up on this and confirmed my conclusion when the boss of the Oversight Group told me the repeat maintenance issue was not within his purview because no federal regulation had been violated. At a medical facility I once almost went into shock (to use a medical term) over the difference between my personal observations and the glowing report the facility had just recently received from a regulatory body. In talking with the employees about how the regulatory review had been conducted, I concluded that the regulators had been industrial tourists, had not gotten in the trenches, had not focused on implementation, were short on observations, and did little pulling of the string. This particular experience of mine was one of the motivators for continuing to pen this book.

Other questions to pursue in diagnosing oversight illnesses include:

1. Are they <u>used by line management</u>? In a number of fields, having an oversight organization is required by federal law. Unfortunately, in some cases, that legal requirement becomes the primary if not the sole reason for its existence. In such cases, the group is formed and then left to its own devices with the satisfaction that the law is being met; however, the overseers are not fully utilized to ensure a high degree of quality. Whether or not these groups are effectively used to improve quality would be evident in the amount of their use by line management. When was the last time an executive asked them to look at something he was worried about? The

degree to which an oversight group is used by line management is a good measure of the value it adds.

2.   Do they <u>know what best in industry is,</u> or are they isolated? Do they have the "exposure" of AACT 2?

3.   Does the oversight staff <u>have a common understanding of what is expected of them</u> by senior management? That is, does management expect them to dog old issues and drive them to resolution, or to identify precursors to prevent problems of significance? Lack of a common understanding of expectations is a frequent contributor to the situation in which a support organization is working hard to support the manager, but the manager is continually dissatisfied. I once concluded that such a disconnect existed when I asked a manager in charge of oversight to tell me his expectations of his staff as I wrote them down. I then distributed copies of what I had written to his staff in a group discussion, only to observe their great surprise.

4.   Do they have <u>credibility with line management</u>? Often this happens when, in frustration at the lack of response, the oversight group continues to report the same issues, but in nastier and nastier terms. This I have found over the years to be a trait of the ill-trained or inexperienced observer, who for some reason, which is probably rooted deeply in his own childhood experiences, has come to believe that if he says something and no action results, then saying it louder, or with more damning adjectives, will result in action. I discuss the importance of providing compelling information later in this book, but for purposes of the discussion here,

suffice to say that to have credibility, these oversight groups must bring value to the line. This can be accomplished only by providing value in their reports -- insight that is helpful to line management in correcting the problems presented. This insight would be developed by using AACTs 14 & 15 [APPLY Y CUBED] and [PULL THE STRING].

OVERSIGHT COMMITTEES

One form of oversight used by some companies is the Oversight Committee. These committees, be they at the Board of Directors level or below, typically consist of experienced senior managers, often from outside the organization. Such committees are typically used by Chief Executives as an aid to "seeing the road." They can and often do add tremendous value; however, as with all functions, they occasionally have shortfalls that need to be addressed. The following techniques can be used in observing these committees:

1. Look for conflicts of interest. Oversight committees are often made up of consultants. By the nature of their business, there is some probability that one or more of these consultants will have done other consulting work for the organization on whose Oversight Committee they serve. If such is the case the stage is unfortunately set for a conflict of interest. I have witnessed a number of occasions where a consultant, carrying out his responsibilities as an Oversight Committee member, either provides directly or implies a judgment on an activity or program that he himself has been involved in developing. The ugliness of the baby on these occasions is likely to be overlooked by the parent. I won't mention the specific instance here in order to avoid embarrassing the individuals involved, but this has actually happened. Readers who pay attention

to issues in the newspapers would surely recognize the resulting incident if I gave specifics. Suffice to say that a significant problem in a facility went uncorrected for a number of years, in part because on oversight body failed to identify the seriousness of the problem. One of the oversight group's consultant members, who was the most qualified to identify the problem, lost sight of its significance because in a separate consulting job, he had worked on resolving the problem and apparently lost his independent oversight of the corrective actions and his ability to recognize these were not aggressive enough.

2.   Look to see that the committee follows up on its comments, but is not prescriptive or direction-giving in those comments. Follow-up is important, but specific actions assigned to organizations by those outside the organization distract the organization and interfere with the priorities of those who are the only ones with enough information to set priorities. This observation can be effectively launched by starting with a review of the committee's minutes or reports.

3.   Review the committee's agendas to gain insight into the value of the committee:

   a.   Are they applying AACT 18 [GET IN THE TRENCHES]? Is there a reasonable amount of time allotted for the committee to be in-facility and are facility visits something other than VIP tours? Surprise requests by the committee to tour facilities can prevent advanced walk-downs of areas and polished doorknobs before the committee tour.

   b.   Is there interaction between the committee and the working and first line supervisor level, that is, where the bottom-line performance occurs? Unlike managers who have vested interest in having their organization look good, those at the working level of an organization are rarely reluctant to talk about the problems they deal with on a daily basis. Not interacting with these people is a great opportunity lost.

c. Is there an absolute minimum of "presentations" to the committee? Canned presentations do little more than allow the presenting managers time to figure out the most positive way to present problems. More importantly, they absorb valuable time that would be better spent out in the trenches or talking with the workforce. If an oversight committee spends most of their time listening to presentations, they will learn what some managers want them to learn. This may not be what they should learn.

d. Does the committee periodically attend routine plant meetings? Attending these meetings allows a view of life at the station – what the standards are; how the communication is; the clarity of management direction; the teamwork among the managers and workers.

e. Is there an evident focus on safety -- nuclear safety, patient safety, or whatever safety is important to the industry involved? Because of the higher level positions those typically serving on Oversight Committees have filled during their careers, there is a tendency to get wrapped up in general management issues. Everyone has an opinion on how to manage and most are more than willing to offer it given the opportunity. However, safety problems can just as well be cloaked in other areas of a more technical nature. Coverage of such areas should be evident in either the agendas or the committee reports.

CORRECTIVE ACTION

Another peripheral but vital function of an organization is that which deals with the handling of corrective action -- the identification of the need for action; the tracking of the actions to completion; and the verification that the actions were effective in correcting whatever problem precipitated them. These attributes are one of the vital signs of any organization. If the process for dealing with corrective action is broken, the organization is broken. Consequently,

44. *OBSERVING HOW WELL AN ORGANIZATION IDENTI-FIES, IMPLEMENTS, AND FOLLOWS UP ON CORRECTIVE ACTION IS LIKE TAKING THE PULSE OF THAT ORGANIZA-TION TO DETERMINE ONE OF ITS VITAL SIGNS*

Looking at the corrective actions of an organization provides a wealth of opportunities to understand how the organization works. Typically, more thought is put into corrective actions than into the actions that were or were not taken initially and that gave birth to whatever problem the corrective actions are now intended to address. Consequently, the observed organization's managers, in defining their corrective action, have already done some work for the observer and all the observer need do is read it. With this in mind, it is useful for the observer to,

45. *DIG INTO CORRECTIVE ACTIONS, BUT DON'T REPACKAGE PROBLEMS AND CALL THEM YOUR FINDINGS*

The above could be a corollary to AACT 41 [DON'T MINE THE SELF-ASSESSMENT DATA] but it is subtly different. A lazy observer (and many consultants) will look at the corrective actions of an organization, describe in reworded terms the problems that required the action to be taken, and provide these to management as his findings regarding the organization. Who could argue with this? By their actions, management has essentially admitted that these are valid problems. But the better question is, what value does this provide to the organization? The answer is "none."

Review each corrective action and make a judgment regarding whether or not it would have been a reasonable action to have taken <u>prior</u> to the problem occurring. A tally or summary of such items can lead to any of a number of hypotheses. As just one example, the action may paint a picture of an organization that is reactive rather than proactive, or one that tries to get by with a minimum of effort and is willing to accept the consequences.

If a historical summary of problems over a period of time shows a number of these are repetitive, then the prospect of ineffective corrective action raises its head. Corrective actions are ineffective for either of only two reasons: either the action was the correct one, but was not taken, or the action was not the correct one. Incorrect actions most frequently result because of an incorrectly defined problem, that is, the action was designed to fix something other than the real problem. The former is easily identified. The latter takes a little more, but not much more, work. It requires delving into the topic of root cause analysis.

46. *BEWARE OF THE DOWNSIDES OF ROOT CAUSE ANALYSIS*

Doing Root Cause Analysis can in itself be one of the

problems an organization has. It can be an anchor that drags down the organization, tying up resources that could otherwise support more warranted actions. Root Cause Analysis has more recently taken on a life of its own. It is now a topic that has made uncountable numbers of consultants rich, yet it means little more than asking why a problem occurred. On nuclear submarines, being the complex machines they were, many problems occurred during operation. Things broke. People made mistakes. When these problems (or incidents as we called them) occurred, we quickly dug into why they occurred, took equally quick action to correct what we found, and moved on. The benefit of this approach was that we were fixing problems of the past while keeping the main focus on the current operation of the submarine. As a Chief Engineer on one of those machines, I can't imagine my reaction if we had a problem and someone told me it would take a month to find out why it happened. I would be expecting an answer of days if not hours. Today many organizations establish large teams, bring in consultants, and set schedules that go out for weeks and sometimes months to determine why something happened. Meanwhile, other problems continue to occur and even more teams and resources are applied. In most cases, finding out why something happened does not require reams of paper with complex diagrams and flow charts. It does require asking people why the problem happened, and then applying reasonable judgment to their responses. For non-technical problems, an effective manager, in a very short time, and typically less than a day, can judge the root cause of a problem and be accurate within the ninety-five plus percent range. Most places would be better off applying their efforts to addressing those initial conclusions rather than spending the inordinate amount of time typically spent by "root cause teams" in researching, flow-charting, and dissecting every aspect of an issue looking for the root cause and every possible underlying contributor. Capturing all of these minor contributors sounds good in theory, but in reality bogs down the organization, especially if multiple root cause investigations get going at the same time. Using a more simplistic approach, one can considerably more quickly reach a conclusion as to the most likely cause of the problem, fix it, and move on. This is an important concept for the observer to understand so that she will not inadvertently drive an organization to deeper and deeper analyses of problems and their causes so that everyone gets wrapped around the axle of the organization and everything comes to a stop, mired in an uncountable number of good but not necessarily needed corrective actions

One other caution on the potential root cause trap is to beware of taking the cause to a higher and higher level until it becomes so general as to be useless. For example, referring back to the example discussed under AACT 14 [APPLY Y CUBED]: The floor may be dirty because the janitor didn't sweep it last night, and the reason the janitor did not sweep it was because the supervisor was not sufficiently involved to ensure the janitor did his job; and the reason the supervisor was not sufficiently involved was because management was not ensuring that he was; and the reason management was not ensuring that the supervisor was involved was because management doesn't really know how to manage. So the floor is dirty because the management doesn't know how to manage. This may, in fact, be true, but every issue in the facility likely has the same root cause -- management doesn't know how to manage. What is the value, when you find the floor dirty, in going to management and telling them they don't know how to manage? Go after the problems that are fixable and work toward resolving the broader issue of management as you accumulate more compelling information. That is,

47. DON'T TRY TO SOLVE WORLD HUNGER

Who defines the "what" and "by-when" for corrective action

is another telling aspect of corrective action. An observer probing into the overall effectiveness of an organization should,

48. *LOOK FOR THE LINE TO BE KEPT RESPONSIBLE -- AND ACCOUNTABLE--FOR DEFINING CORRECTIVE ACTIONS AND THEIR PRIORITIES*

If this is not the case, consider it to be a valid problem worthy of bringing to the attention of executive management. No one knows better than the people running an organization what will correct a problem and what won't. These line managers are the same ones who best understand the numerous other activities that compete for their time and thus are the best ones to set the priority and therefore define the time by which the action will be taken. I have found that oversight groups or other non-line organizational entities only define the What and By-When in dysfunctional organizations. One important reason for this is that by relieving line management of the responsibility for defining what is to be done about a problem and when it is to be done by, one relieves that line management of the accountability for correcting the problem. This is not to say that oversight groups cannot or should not be heard in any disagreement with what the line intends to do.

In looking at how any organization defines, tracks, and then closes corrective actions, it is important to recognize, that just like garden vegetables,

49. *EFFECTIVE CORRECTIVE ACTION EFFORTS WILL ONLY FLOURISH IN A FOSTERING ENVIRONMENT*

An effective observer will look for this environment. Look for the organization to have clear expectations in place so that the staff understands that problems are expected to be self-identified before they are identified by any outside organization. Should some outside review find a problem not already known to the staff, that staff should feel badly, and they should have the urge to immediately look into why they had not identified the problem themselves. This is a sign of a healthy organization. A good environment for corrective action also is one in which it is not only expected but also strongly and proactively encouraged to identify problems. Consequently, an observer should also look to see that management has made it clear that problem reporting will not be accompanied by discipline (except in cases of willful misdeeds or gross negligence). Mixing disciplinary action with problem reporting is the quickest and most sure way to "chill" the environment so that problems will remain unreported.

The environment of a facility will often be reflected in the number of problems self-identified. I once worked at a facility where the message that management had inadvertently sent to the workforce was, "We have no money to fix problems." At this same facility, there was a clear record of having no problems with the hundreds of indicators that were monitored in the facility. Then the message was changed to "Money is tight; it always is; but we, the management, want to know what the problems are and we expect you, the workers, to report them." Shortly after this message was effectively communicated, 250 instrument deficiencies were reported.

Most workers in the United States are very hard working, intelligent, motivated and creative individuals. The general work ethic is geared to getting the job done. With the wrong message from management, these positive traits can work to a disadvantage. I recall another case at a high hazard production facility in which the "need to cut cost" message was clearly received by the workforce. At this facility, the workers subsequently identified that the circuit breaker feeding electric current to a very large rotating machine was undersized. When the large current needed to move the machine from a stationary condition to a rotating condition began to flow, the undersized circuit breaker would trip. Recognizing that replacement of the breaker would entail a huge expense, the workers innovatively came up with their own solution. They implemented the practice of manually shutting the circuit breaker, allowing current to start flowing, then immediately reopening the breaker (before the high current caused it to trip). They even came up with their own term for this. They called it "bumping" the machine. Once they had "bumped" the machine, they would then reshut the breaker now that the inertia of the machine had been overcome and it had begun to roll from the initial shot of current. With the high starting current no longer required, the machine would then continue to operate. This practice remained in place for years. Fortunately, the machine was never called upon in an emergency to start automatically. Had it been so called on, this clever work-around would not have been available and an important piece of equipment would not have been available when needed -- a condition that had existed for years because the work environment did not foster effective corrective action.

As with all processes that are observed, it is important for the observer to work fast and cover a lot of ground in a short period of time when observing the handling of corrective actions. Otherwise, the look at corrective action will be incomplete. One way to work fast is to not waste time looking at material unnecessarily. A great place to apply this principle is in reviewing an organization's response to problems that are identified -- either self-identified or identified by an outside organization. In short,

50. *DON'T WASTE TIME LOOKING AT RESPONSES TO A PROBLEM UNLESS THAT PROBLEM IS FIRST VERIFIED TO STILL EXIST*

This seems like common sense and I wouldn't even say it here if I had not seen uncountable numbers of observers laboring over a facility's responses to "findings," and then criticizing some of the actions taken, when in fact the problem had already been corrected and the staff of the facility was asking the observer the legitimate question, So what?

Another common fault in the corrective action processes of organizations, particularly those that are trying hard to improve, is taking too many corrective actions. Form a mental picture of quicksand. Quicksand is nothing more than sand that is fully saturated with water such that the friction between the sand particles is reduced. It is not the sticky stuff that the movies would have us believe sucks a person down and eventually envelopes them regardless of their actions. In fact, if a person were to tread into quicksand and then do nothing, they would just float in the sand. Not unless they continually struggled would they continue to sink deeper. The analogy is a good one:

51. *TAKING TOO MANY CORRECTIVE ACTIONS IS QUICKSAND IN THE MANAGEMENT JUNGLE*

Managers can and often do lay out so many corrective actions, the number of which are proportional to the seriousness of the problem that precipitated them, that they literally sink as they struggle to manage and then close all of the actions they have developed.

One observation technique that can be used to identify whether or not management is treading into this quicksand follows. Select any problem in any corrective action process and consider what caused the problem to occur. Then do a simple "bean count" of those corrective actions planned to be taken that will not affect the cause of the original problem. Unarguably, these latter actions may be "good" actions; taking them may benefit the organization in one way or another. As an example, who would argue that revising a procedure to make it clearer is not a good thing to do -- even though the procedure's lack of clarity had nothing to do with the problem being addressed? The real question to ask is, How do these "good to do" things fit into the priorities of the organization? The situation is exacerbated by the fact that these ancillary actions often take on the importance of the problem with which they are associated. As a result, if a very significant problem occurs, an uncountable number of corrective actions will result. Many if not most of these will have nothing to do with the problem that occurred. All will be handled as being important with due dates assigned accordingly; and the end result will be another bunch of "stuff" for management to do -- the quicksand that envelopes them and ironically prevents them from getting on with fixing the real contributors to that problem.

ACTION PLANS

Because it is geared to actions rather than results, the term "action plan" in itself has the potential to do all a disservice. A good observer will:

52. *LOOK FOR "RESULTS PLANS" NOT ACTION PLANS*

I can't count the number of times I have interacted with people who were satisfied with and consequently closed "action plan" items when the actions for the items were completed. They did this while not having a clue as to whether or not the actions had resulted in anything that was substantive and related to the original reason for the action plan. I once inquired at a medical facility about what had been done to improve the behaviors related to safety at the facility, a need that was self recognized by their management.

The responder proudly referred to an action plan and the large number of items on it that had already been completed. Having first observed the facility and concluded that the behaviors still needed considerable work, I pulled the string on the action plan by selecting one item, "Purchase a new copying machine." The item had in fact been completed, and there the machine sat. The purpose of the action plan item was in no way being met. In defense of the facility, their intentions were good. They had "hoped" to use the machine to put out more communications on, and thereby increase the understanding of, the importance of patient safety and how the various caregivers could contribute to it. However, the item on the plan said "Purchase a new copying machine," and contained none of the background information or description of the hoped for use. Consequently, the intended action remained just as it was referred to, "hoped" for but not completed.

Another common problem with action plans is that they tend to get very large and full of irrelevant actions. Remember that,

53. A BIG PLAN ISN'T NECESSARILY A GOOD PLAN

People often apply more effort to coming up with actions to put into action plans than to ensuring that the actions that do go into the plan will really fix the problem the plan was intended to address. To look for this common malady, an observer should scrutinize each item in any action plan reviewed, and ensure that the action addresses at least some aspect of the problem. Select some completed actions and look for either some measurement or focused self-assessment to determine if the actions effectively addressed the issues they were intended to address.

The best approach that I have seen (and used) to preclude

the above problem is first, specifically define each issue you are trying to correct; lay out actions to address it; following completion of those actions, do a focused self-assessment to determine if the issue still exists; then, if it does, define additional actions to be taken. In turn, following these actions, again do a self-assessment to determine if the issue is really fixed. The observer can use this approach as a mental benchmark when reviewing an action plan.

Another common fault in the use of action plans involves the often misunderstood concept that,

54. *"DONE" REALLY MEANS DONE, THAT IS, DONE-DONE*

To emphasize this point to our employees in one organization in which I worked, we referred to tasks that were really done, that is done completely and correctly and verified to have been done, as "done-done." Whenever an assignment or task was reported as "done," the responsible manager would query, "done – done?" This served as a good reminder to reinforce what was expected for completed action items.

People generally operate with the best of intentions, but in the world of reality, intentions don't get you anything. Action plan developers unfortunately don't often enough put the effort into clearly defining the actions they would like to have accomplished by their plan. For example, what does the item, often found in action plans, "Develop a program" really mean? Does it mean develop a program, put it in a folder, and file it on your shelf? Does it mean develop the program, issue a document describing it, and then hope it gets implemented? Does it mean actually implement the program? And how would one ascertain that the program is, in fact, implemented? These are the thoughts that would well serve the action plan developer as he goes about his business. Unfortunately, such is not often the case. However, even with the best of plans, disconnects are frequently the case -- disconnects between the plan developer; the manager responsible for the plan; and the doer of the actions.

Take any action plan and select about three items. Considering the thoughts above, select the items most likely to be suspect. Track down the doers and ask them what specifically they did to complete the items, or what they will consider to be "done" for the item. Then ask the manager or managers responsible what these same items mean. Hopefully your test will prove me wrong, but I'll bet on a disconnect. And since action plans are often used to fix problems, I'll also bet the original problem is still there as well.

Again, applying the concept of exposure to the best, referred to in the opening of this book, under AACT 2 [EXPERIENCE, EXPOSURE ,AND ENERGY ARE THE REQUISITES OF A GOOD OBSERVER], what do the best organizations do to preclude having tasks that are "done" not really done-done? Require the doer to document his basis for closure of the item. This gives the person in charge a chance to agree or not with the closure actions. It also allows for independent oversight of those items selected as most important for success of the plan.

CONDITION OF FACILITIES AND EQUIPMENT

The biggest problem with the topic of "condition" is that many people talk about and freely use the term, recognize the importance of it, but tend to forget what it really means. I can't count the number of people, who when asked what was being done to improve the physical condition of a facility, talked about either extensive effort to clean the facility, the attitudes of the people, or about some other activities that may have been indirectly related to but were not in themselves descriptive of the condition of the facility.

55. *THE VALUE OF A USED CAR DEPENDS ON THE CONDITION OF THE CAR, NOT THE INTENTIONS OF THE OWNER*

It should go without saying, to the type of person likely to be reading this book, that the condition of a facility is important because if the physical condition of a place is poor, the likelihood of it operating to produce whatever it is supposed to produce is low. In some more potentially hazardous environments, such as chemical plants, healthcare facilities, or power generating stations, particularly nuclear stations, there is even more importance placed on the condition of the equipment, because its failure can bring about disastrous effects in itself.

Physical condition is one topic, more than any other, where a focus on results is essential to have a meaningful discussion. When asked about the condition of a facility, people often want to talk about the training that the maintenance personnel are getting, or about the new program just put in place to visually identify any deficiency in the facility so that it can be worked more expeditiously.

I have also found it useful in coaching observers to remind them that the condition of a facility or of a piece of equipment consists both of the "visible condition" and the "non-visible condition." The real condition of the item is the sum of both. If a tire on a used car is flat, or the floor tiles of a hospital operating room are worn and rough allowing for the buildup of infectious material, these conditions are clearly visible and part of the items' condition. But just as true, if the car has a timing belt that has not been replaced as recommended by the manufacturer, or has not had regular oil changes, then the condition of that car is poor but not readily visible. Likewise, if the electronics and other complex equipment in a hospital operating room are not well maintained, the condition of that room may as well be poor and a threat to patient safety, even though its appearance is fine. For example, not long ago, a patient in a hospital outside of the United States died after otherwise uncomplicated surgery to treat two aneurysms. A microscope had failed during the operation and became stuck on full zoom, making completion of the surgery difficult. The microscope had been faulty for some time before the operation and no effective action had been taken to fix it. This kind of condition would not be visible unless the observer happened to be present during one of the failures. The good observer will consider both the visible and the non-visible aspects when assessing the condition of a facility.

My advice to anyone tasked with assessing condition of a facility, is to put yourself in the frame of mind of a person about to buy a used car. Then do your probing the same way you would if you were trying to ascertain the value of the car. Hopefully you are not one of those who are easily fooled by a car recently cleaned or "detailed." Given that a spotless, clean smelling car can be naturally attractive, cleanliness does not reflect "condition," and may in fact be a purposely positioned façade for a poorly maintained machine. You would be interested in whether or not the various parts can reliably perform the function for which they were designed. Does it have worn tires? Will important equipment that is normally passive, such as the horn, work when it is called on to work? Has periodic maintenance been performed regularly, such as the oil and filter changed? Has it had recurring problems, such as the battery periodically going dead? You might also be interested in other things such as how well trained are the mechanics who worked on the car? How well kept are the records on the car? But remember that although the responses to these questions may give a positive impression of practices that are consistent with a car in good condition, they do <u>not</u> indicate a measure of the actual current condition and thus the value of the car. When on a mission to observe the condition of a car (or a facility), do not allow positive impressions of matters not <u>directly</u> related to that condition to influence your judgment.

CHAPTER 6
WATCHING THE PEOPLE
(SUPPOSEDLY) IN CHARGE

Terms such as supervisor, manager, executive, and even the term, management, can mean different things to different people. I have here defined the hierarchy of those terms as I use them in referring to those in charge. Not to say this is any more accurate a definition than that provided by anyone else, but it will help to ensure a consistency in communication within this discussion of the topic. Graphically, the hierarchy and portions of it that I refer to as "management" are described in figure 2.

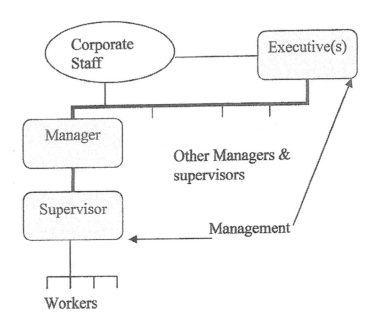

Fig 2. Definition of "management"

Executives are those at the level of Vice President or Director and above, who are directly in the chain of command for facility operation. The term "executive" will apply to these individuals regardless of whether they are located at the facility or the corporate office. Supervisors are those who are below the manager level and carry the prime responsibility for the performance of the workers reporting to them. Typically, supervisors are at the direct interface between managers and the workers. Managers are all of those in between the executives and the supervisors, recognizing that in many organizations, there are multiple levels of managers.

Within the context of this definition, when I use the term "management," I refer to those at all of the levels above the front line worker.

There is a sea of management books that provide an almost infinite amount of information on management techniques, strategies, and styles. Much of this information unfortunately is written by theorists who have never themselves practiced the art (or science if you prefer) of management. Other of this information is written by managers who tend to favor one style or technique that may or may not work in an organization different from or staffed with personalities different from those in the organization upon which the advocate bases his advice.

One of my most valuable learnings as I observed hundreds of organizations and uncountable numbers of executive personalities and styles has to do with the self-generated question: Why do some in management, who have proven themselves to be effective in one well-run organization, fail when placed in another equally well-run organization? I concluded that management is like chemistry. The combination of people, personalities and styles that make up management, is not unlike a chemical solution. Every ingredient (or every individual) can be useful and effective in its (or his) own right, but when mixed with another ingredient, that is also useful and effective in its own right, or when placed in the wrong environment, can result in a corrosive, volatile, or even an explosive mixture. Similarly, when a person with a limited duffle of management abilities is mixed properly with another who also has a limited but different set of management abilities (or characteristics), the two can together constitute a highly effective solution. For example, a manager with strong accountability traits mixed with a manager who is heavily people-oriented and more democratically minded, can together in the right environment, form a powerful team that makes best use of the strongest characteristics of each ingredient. However, put one of these in the solution in a manner or amount that allows it to overpower the other, and you have the making of a volatile solution in which one of the ingredients is destined to fail.

To apply this learning, all an observer needs to do is be aware of it and not get caught up in trying to judge individual personalities and techniques or management styles. Instead, apply AACT 1 [THINK PERFORMANCE BASED] and consider only the final result. I recall performing assessment work at two very large organizations. One of these was run (literally) by a CEO who seemed to understand and prefer only draconian tactics. Accountability throughout the organization was high, monetary compensation was equally high in order to stem the flow of deserters, but so was the level of fear and uncertainty -- uncertainty as to whether or not a person would have a job the following day. The second organization was considerably less stressed. This CEO set clear expectations that his organization would foster a kinder, gentler work environment. Accountability was important, but equally important was encouraging employees to have fun, enjoy their work, and to support each other as a team. Firing was a concept infrequently discussed and even less frequently applied. Which of these organizations would you guess was more likely to achieve success and maintain it over the long term? If you guessed it would be the latter organization, you would be wrong. If you guessed it would be the former organization, you would also be wrong. Both achieved and were widely recognized for maintaining high levels of performance, in terms of productivity, efficiency, and most importantly, safety. The performance of both continued to excel over time -- at least for the fifteen years that I was familiar with them. What is the point? As an observer of performance, stick with looking for the bottom line <u>results</u> -- how is the company performing? Don't get caught up in trying to analyze styles of individuals before seeing first whether or not the results warrant analysis of the styles. Many factors drive performance of a company, and management styles and personalities are rarely among these.

ALIGNMENT

One example of a driving factor, and a most influential one, has to do with the degree to which everyone in the company is marching in the same direction. Regardless of styles or personalities, an organization will go where its boss tells it to go, if the boss' message is clear and frequently reinforced. Consequently, it is the job of the executive in charge to tell the organization where to go and to ensure that all understand the message and comply with it. This is alignment -- alignment of all in the organization with the CEO's provided direction. Alignment is an attribute that an effective observer would first look for in an organization. One would begin to look for alignment by finding out if the person in charge has told the organization where to go. In the absence of a clear and regularly reinforced message, an organization will attempt to move in the direction of the strongest driving force. If there is not a powerful and overriding force, then there either will be no driving force, in which case the organization will remain stationary and stagnant, or there will be multiple forces provided by any number of other well-intentioned and strong-minded leaders. These strong personalities likely will have varying ideas, and consequently the organization will either move in random fashion or be buffeted by opposing forces and essentially get nowhere.

56. *IT TAKES MANAGEMENT ALIGNMENT TO MOVE AN ORGANIZATION IN A CONSISTENT DIRECTION*

Observing the degree of alignment among management and the workforce involves little more than asking the boss a few fundamental questions, to understand where she wants the organization to go and how she expects it to get there. These questions might include, What are the top three priorities of the organization? What are the three biggest problems the organization faces? And, what do you expect managers, supervisors, and workers to be doing <u>right now</u> to address those issues? Then, compare the manager's responses with the responses of others to the same or similar questions, down through the various levels of the organization, including the working level. I recall the senior manager at one facility essentially giving me the look of a wild animal caught in the headlights of an automobile when I asked him what the focus of his facility was. After an embarrassing delay, one of his subordinates responded to the question with a list of items. During this response by the subordinate, the senior manager said, "I better take notes." There shouldn't be any surprise to learn this organization was floundering with multiple agendas driven by those with the strongest personalities. Remember that those with the most driving personalities don't always have the greatest experience or seniority in the organization and may therefore be the least capable of driving the company in the right direction. As one other example, the following were my notes on the top priorities of the senior executive at one organization, as compared to the stated priorities of the senior oversight manager for that same organization. The Oversight Manager was responsible for providing the senior executive with a view of what was happening at his facility from an oversight perspective:

Senior Executive's list:

- Ensuring his operations staff would make conservative decisions when faced with options in the middle of the night

- Control of work performed at the facility by outside groups, such as contracted labor

- Material Condition of the equipment

Senior Oversight Manager's list

- Reduction of errors made by the workforce

- Improvement of efficiency in the organization

- Material Condition of the equipment

At least they were in synchronism on <u>one</u> item. It made for some interesting discussion to talk with them about what was said and emphasized about material condition that was not said or emphasized in driving for positive change on the other items that gave the senior executive concern. In this case, both individuals were well intentioned. The senior executive had mentally framed the issues that were of greatest concern to him; however, he had not communicated them to his managers in order to achieve alignment. They consequently were marching off in their own directions.

Another opportunity for checking alignment exists when executive management has come up with some of those catchy words and phrases that executives often come up with after reading the latest management book. One of these I recall was an organization that had launched an improvement effort using the phrase, "Best of Class." The hope was that the phrase would motivate the workforce to move ahead. I took that phrase and tested knowledge of it down through the organization. My test provided some interesting insight. At the employee level, where the work was actually being done, most had never heard the phrase, even though the improvement effort had been launched some several months before. Many of those who had heard the phrase had no idea what it meant. At the middle manager and supervisory levels, there was less ignorance of the phrase, but considerable disparity among the opinions of what it meant. Most interestingly, only a handful of people at any level could articulate what they were <u>doing</u> differently as a result of the improvement effort or since the phrase had been promulgated as a goal. If you're using one of these catch phrases, you may want to do your own check for alignment.

How is alignment achieved in effective organizations? I recall several companies using a simple method that I have also used successfully in this regard. I provide it here only as an example of a type of method that an observer could look for (or could look for the absence of). The method is fundamental and involves three steps:

1. <u>Get the message out.</u> Define the top priorities or the key performance areas in which one wants the organization to move ahead. Then relentlessly drive on communicating and reinforcing the message. Print the priorities and expectations for implementing them on cards and give a card to each employee. Require that the cards be carried with the employee at all times he is at work. Put the information on posters throughout the facility. Include it in every newsletter; refer to it in every announcement. Include words in the message that

will have meaning to the workforce rather than lofty words that for some reason managers tend to use. (Are you getting the point that I mean getting the message out any and every way you can?) Use actionable statements. For example, at one facility where we wanted to improve the adherence to policies, one of the statements on the cards we provided was, "I will refer to written policy whenever in doubt and will inform my supervisor if a policy cannot be adhered to."

2. <u>Reinforce the message.</u> Hold supervisors accountable for reinforcing at every opportunity the actions needed to support the focus areas. Give periodic quizzes on the items with token rewards for those who do well. Require all in management to ask the workers and supervisors what the priorities and expected actions are at every chance they get.

3. <u>Insist on actions as well as words.</u> Require detailed strategies or plans with specific actions to achieve progress in each of the focus areas. Translate the promulgated words into actions so the effort doesn't become just one more cheerleading session. Keep the work force apprised of progress to help build momentum.

4. <u>Be relentless.</u> Drive on these focus areas until you're absolutely convinced you're overdoing it -- and then drive harder.

Just because an organization is not using the above method, does not make it wrong. Remember AACT 10 [DIFFERENT IS NOT WRONG]. However, an observer can and should determine what means or methods are being used to achieve alignment. Alignment is not something that just happens spontaneously. If nothing specific is being done to achieve it, it likely is not being achieved.

As a side note here, don't look for alignment as an end in itself. Just because an organization is aligned, doesn't mean a thing, if they're aligned in the wrong direction. I recall one large organization that had been performing pretty well but had decided to pursue the Deming award for quality. The degree of the company's alignment in this effort was truly amazing. I have never seen anything like it, either before then or since. At every level, all the way down through the most junior worker, people were perfectly aligned on the actions needed to win the award. The workforce was even frequently heard reciting the sayings of their Japanese quality coaches hired to assist them in winning the award. People were walking around saying things like, "The man who chases two rabbits seldom catches one." Unfortunately, this was an electrical power generating business and not an award winning business. While they were memorizing sayings, developing measures, and requiring the majority of the management team's time to be spent in meetings and training on quality techniques, they lost sight of the sole reason for the company's existence. While they were focusing on the award, their business performance went south. It was not until the CEO was removed and alignment was achieved on the safe and efficient generation of power that the company recovered. There are other cases of airplane crews being perfectly aligned on something other than a safe flight path as they executed the deadly maneuver of "controlled flight into terrain," an exercise that constitutes a large percentage of airline accidents

ORGANIZATIONAL STRUCTURE

A truism that should be evident in the preceding discussion, but that is often either not recognized or not accepted, is that the performance of an organization is heavily dependent on the performance of management. No surprise there, right? Then did you ever wonder (as I have) why one of the first things to get changed following the occurrence of problems in an organization is often the organization chart? There is no argument that some organizational structures allow managers to be more efficient than others, and that some structures may support better communication than others. But cause significant problems, organizational structures do not. Think about it. Structure doesn't <u>do</u> anything! Structure can't perform well or otherwise! If there's a problem in an organization, structure didn't cause it! Managers caused it! If you want to fix the problem, fix the managers not the structure. I have never seen a new organization chart fix a problem. Consultants often have criticisms to offer on organizational structure. The primary reason for this is that these criticisms are easy to make. There is no dearth of opinion on how an organization should be structured, and rarely is the opinion that the structure is fine as is. You don't even need to know what the company does to offer this opinion. You certainly don't have to go to their facilities, much less get out in the trenches, before you offer an opinion on structure. To avoid having observers who worked for me go chasing down the cold rabbit trails of organizational structure, I promulgated and reinforced on a regular basis, the concept that,

57. ANY ORGANIZATION WILL WORK

Some structures may be a little better than others, but any structure will work -- if the managers in that structure are capable and do their jobs. Applying this concept forces the management observer to dig deeper and identify the real problems and to find out what managers need to <u>do</u> differently to either preclude or correct a problem. Keep this thought in mind as you watch the evening news and notice how frequently government organizations restructure to fix problems. The following is one example I recently read on the internet: Congressional testimony on performance problems at nuclear weapons facilities operated by the Department of Energy listed six significant weaknesses. These included:

- The "longstanding concern" of weaknesses in important processes
- Weaknesses in the management of corrective action
- Weaknesses in line management reviews that were not rigorous and thereby lead to recurring deficiencies
- Weaknesses that had been identified in past inspections
- Progress that had been inconsistent and sporadic

A key element in the response to the above review was, "... reorganizing the management structure." Which of those items do you think the structure caused in the first place?

CONSISTENT ADHERENCE TO EXPECTATIONS

One characteristic symptomatic of an organization that has difficulty achieving the highest levels of performance is an environment in which each individual worker is allowed to decide for himself whether or not he needs to adhere to the expectations promulgated in that organization. This kind of environment is considerably more prevalent than one would expect. Because of this, it is important for the management observer to look at the consistency of adherence to expectations.

58. *CONSISTENT ADHERENCE TO EXPECTATIONS IS A HALL MARK OF A TOP PERFORMING ORGANIZATION*

This concept is valid regardless of the importance of the expectations -- for a reason I will explain shortly.

To understand how an organization -- and thus its management-- works, observe how consistently management expectations are reinforced. And by this I mean <u>ALL</u> expectations. If at first you don't believe this, bear with me until I complete my point and the basis for it. If management, for whatever reason, decides that it is important and therefore sets an expectation that every employee is to walk around with a banana on his head, then it really is important to that organization's long term performance that employees walk around with bananas on their heads. A useful and illustrative way to think about this point is to consider a graph, with "importance" on the abscissa and "adherence" on the ordinate. See figure 3, which is an illustration of subjective but empirical data based on years of observation.

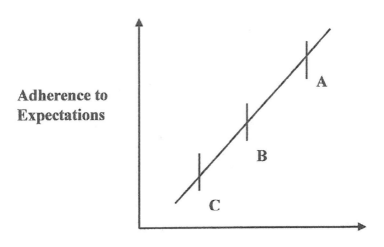

Adherence to Expectations

Importance of Expectations

Fig 3. Adherence to Expectations (typical)

When looking at many organizations, one too often finds that there is, unfortunately, a direct correlation between the importance or perceived importance of an expectation and the degree to which that expectation is met. For example, if there is an expectation to not touch an exposed and energized, high voltage wire, few would disagree with the importance of adhering to this expectation and consequently, few if any would not adhere to it. The same could be said about the expectation that a surgeon is to wear gloves during surgery. No reasonable surgeon in a normal environment would question the importance of or not adhere to this expectation. Consider both of these examples to be near the point "A" on figure 3 -- high importance; high level of adherence. Contrarily, if there is an expectation to wear a piece of safety equipment in an area where there is clearly no safety hazard, to wear a hardhat in a normal office space for example (or to walk around with a banana on your head) this would quickly be seen as foolish by the workforce and adherence would be low. The same could also be said for an expectation to document a piece of information that workers see no need to document. These examples would be shown on figure 3 as points in the area "C" -- low importance and low adherence. One might make an argument that this graph so far only reflects common sense brought into play by the wisdom of the workforce. But consider examples that represent neither obviously frivolous requirements nor ones that carry with them consequences of life or death. These would fall somewhere in the area of "B", neither exceptionally important nor unimportant, and thus might experience a modicum of adherence. This category might include the expectation that a nurse in a hospital wash his hands before and after touching a patient. An experienced nurse with more work than can be accomplished in the time allowed, might conclude based on his own experience (and incorrectly) that this hand-washing does not really need to be done in every case. In these "area B" cases, there likely would be considerably greater variation in the perceived importance and consequently in the degree of adherence. The data, of course, would not fall on a discreet line, but would rather be more like a cloud of data points. However, the graph would definitely show a slope as indicated in the illustration. Now think about what this sliding scale of adherence based on perceived importance means in practical terms -- it's like getting your workers together and telling them what you expect them to do; how you expect them to do it, and by when you expect them to have it done; then concluding your directions to them with the caveat that they should go back to their work space, think about whether or not they believe each of your expectations is important, and then adhere to only those they consider important! This sounds facetious, but it happens on a regular basis in many organizations -- too many.

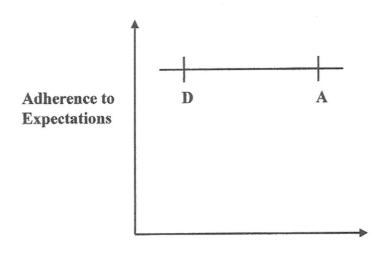

Fig 4. Adherence to Expectations (optimum)

Well run organizations typically have a performance profile that is horizontal, like that in figure 4. In this flattened spectrum, all expectations are considered, at least to some degree, to be important and are expected to be adhered to -- consistently. Even the lesser important expectations, such as details of a dress code, which might fall in the area of point D on the graph, see a high degree of adherence. If an expectation is determined to be unimportant (like our banana example), it is eliminated. Organizations that expect and insist on high standards in meeting expectations across the spectrum of importance achieve a much higher level of success in reducing shortfalls in meeting more important expectations, and thus in reducing serious events.

THE PEOPLE FACTOR

59. *NOT PAYING ATTENTION TO PEOPLE PERFORMANCE IS NOT PAYING ATTENTION TO PERFORMANCE*

If a facility has a problem with people not performing the way they are expected to, then the organization has a supervisor problem. It's a direct correlation. Supervisors are a conduit between managers and the workforce. Yet it continually amazes me how little attention organizations give this most important role of supervisors. If there is a common weakness in supervisors, it is in them not seeing themselves as being accountable for the performance of their people. They more often take a myopic view, focusing only on the technical aspects of the specific work for which they are responsible. I once observed an organization that was having problems with workers making mistakes, not cleaning up after themselves, and not working efficiently. All of these shortfalls were either contributing to or symptomatic of the overall poor performance of the facility. In talking to the supervisors about what might be causing the poor performance, it struck me that at no time in their remarks or responses to my questions did they mention anything about the performance of the workers. I asked them about the worker's break room, which would make a pig sty look like a Martha Stewart-made-over room;

the typical dress of the workers, which usually included either a dirty tee shirt or a shirt with some lewd remark on it; the worker's locker room, which was at best a fire hazard because it wasn't even large enough to store the winter clothing the people wore to work; and the constant complaining I heard from the supervisors just below the level of those to whom I was speaking. All of these items caught the supervisors cold! They were aware of the conditions but just hadn't given them any thought. When pressed, the most I could get out of these supervisors was that the items I mentioned just were not a priority! "Not on the radar screen" they said. On the other hand, the technical expertise of these supervisors was nothing less than impressive. I probed their familiarity with a number of equipment problems that I knew existed from my extensive preparation for this visit. They could tell me, in excruciating detail, about every aspect of every technical problem that I brought up. But they were ignoring the <u>people</u> issues -- the high use of overtime; the inaccuracy of the work schedules; the poor conditions of the work environment; the poor retention of experienced workers. The facility's problems stemmed from the performance of the people, not the performance of the equipment, yet the latter was on what the emphasis was placed.

My strong belief in the above concept has at least part of its roots back in my time working with nuclear submarines. Again, under the tutelage of the forces of Admiral H.G. Rickover, we operated under the concept that there were no such things as equipment problems, or process problems, or procedure problems. There were only people problems. If a piece of equipment malfunctioned, it had to have been designed, or operated, or maintained, improperly. There were no other possibilities and all of these activities had been performed by people. If a problem was at first thought to be a procedure or process deficiency, it was soon remembered that it was a person who wrote that procedure or designed that process. This approach has downsides because it can foster an environment in which a primary activity is "going after people." I recall the often repeated joke in the nuclear submarine force that the prize for 1st place was nothing, and every single person worked as hard as they possibly could, twenty four hours a day if necessary to win it. The reason for striving for a first place prize of nothing was that the prize for second place was a kick in the butt. Twenty five years in the civilian business community has caused me to temper my thoughts on this subject, but I retained an appreciation for the benefits that can come from concentrating on people rather than inanimate objects when performance improvement is the goal. A good observer will be equally sensitive to this same point.

THE MANAGEMENT MODEL

A question that is often asked about management is, how good are they? An organization I once worked for was asked to come up with a reasonably objective way of determining an answer to this question. In response to the challenge we first expanded the question to, How good are they AT WHAT? We then set about defining WHAT. After much brainstorming on what seemed at first to be a simple question, we came up with the following: It is well recognized that managers and supervisors do many things, but in carrying out their most important function, which is interacting with the workforce, the job of managers and supervisors can be boiled down to the following: they tell people what to do; they then determine if the people did what they were expected to do; they make judgments of the quality of what was done; and they then interact with the workers to provide feedback and further direction. Following this, the circle continues and additional direction is provided, either in that assignment, or on the next one. This can be visualized in the model shown in figure 5.

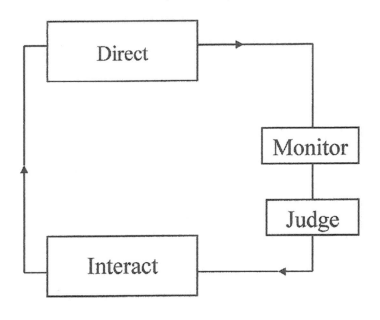

Fig 5. Management Model

DIRECT -- is the step in which the person in charge tells the worker what to do. In a facilitative work environment, this is equally true, except that the input of the workforce is solicited, given fair consideration, and factored into the direction. The description applies as well when workers are "empowered" because management retains the accountability for the final product and consequently de facto gives direction for the work to be done.

MONITOR -- is the step in which the manager or supervisor determines if the worker did what she was expected to do. Monitoring can be accomplished by many means, but the primary ones are going into the work areas and seeing for herself, or reviewing numerical indicators or other written reports.

JUDGE -- is the step in which, having seen what the worker has done, the supervisor makes a judgment as to how well the task has been done. Mentally or otherwise he compares the completed work with other completed work he has seen accomplished or perhaps with work that he himself has done in earlier years.

INTERACT -- is the step in which the manager interacts with the worker (or supervisor) to give positive feedback if the work is done well; to coach if best effort was exerted but expectations for final results were not achieved; or to hold accountable or make it clear to the person that her performance did not meet expectations, if that is the response warranted.

MONITORING BY SUPERVISORS

Since this book is about observing, and I have already provided my opinion that observing is the primary and most effective method of monitoring, I provide the following as a personally experienced example of how monitoring can be assessed.

I once was involved with an organization that recognized its supervisors were not spending a sufficient amount of time in the workplace, monitoring the performance of and coaching the employees. To address this problem, management of the facility had put in place a requirement for supervisors to conduct some specific number of observations of their direct reports while they were working, and to document these observations -- a practice not uncommon in the nuclear power industry. Shortly after implementation of this requirement, senior management proudly proclaimed the success of the effort based on the fact that "over 1800 observations had been conducted in the previous three months and these had provided some really useful information." Being more interested in the half of the glass that was empty rather than the half that the manager described as full, I practiced AACT 16 [GO SEE FOR YOURSELF]. I read and analyzed the most recent 850 of the observations. This took considerable time, but was worth the effort. It also reinforced in my mind the importance of the "energy" element of AACT 2 [EXPERIENCE, EXPOSURE, AND ENERGY ARE THE REQUISITE ATTRIBUTES OF A GOOD OBSERVER.] My review led me to the conclusion that the manager was absolutely correct. At least 1800 observations had been conducted. And "some really useful information" had been provided. However, I could find only <u>three</u> items that might be considered in this "really useful" category! I also noted the following:

- Eighty four percent of the observations had no comments, thus indicating essentially excellent performance. This was in striking contrast to other reports within the facility that indicated a rash of personnel errors with an underlying theme of complacency during routine evolutions.

- If the observations with comments that were either non-substantial or were constructive and critical but unrelated to the observable performance of the workers (comments related to cleanliness and storage for example) were excluded from my count, then the percent of observations indicating excellent performance went to 96 – even more striking.

My follow-up on this information included discussions with the supervisors and watching them perform their observations. I eventually concluded this observation effort, as it was being conducted at the time, was not an effective use of supervisor time. Reasons for the minimal amount of useful results fell into three categories: a propensity to identify and document "grey information," a lack of supervisor awareness of management expectations that these observations were to be critical, and a reluctance to identify performance issues involving people with whom the supervisors had a close working relationship. Detailed analysis of any internally conducted observation results, along with follow-up, is generally a useful tool for any observer to apply.

Returning to the management model and its application,

60. *BE SENSITIVE TO WHAT THOSE IN CHARGE ARE SUPPOSED TO DO AND OBSERVE THEM DOING IT*

The model in Figure 5 provides a good means for an observer to group the information she has collected when observing the performance of those in charge. Do the supervisors provide adequate DIRECTION? What do they say? How do they say it? To whom do they say it? How is it received? Is it understood? Do they MONITOR? How frequently do they get into the work area? What do they do when in the area? Can the workers recall the last time they received feedback as a result of their supervisor's monitoring? Do they have the experience and exposure to JUDGE? Do they know what good looks like? When was the last time they visited some other facility? Are they familiar with best in the industry?

The management model also provides a good tool for discussion with both middle level managers and supervisors. These people typically want to do a good job, and are generally quite candid in the discussion of their activities. This model can be used to have a group discussion with managers or supervisors, during which they are asked to rate themselves as far as what are the strongest and weakest elements of their performance relative to this model. This is a particularly useful tool when, for comparative purposes, it is applied to several layers of management and supervision within the same authority chain. I once had a most interesting discussion about the performance of supervisors with a group of managers, using this model. The managers rated the supervisors particularly poorly in the area of providing feedback to the workers and holding them accountable. When I discussed the exercise and the resultant rating with the supervisors, I found that not only did the supervisors see themselves in a generally more positive light than their managers had, but they were also amazed to find out their bosses saw such shortfalls in their performance! My conclusions in this case included the fact that the managers were not communicating their expectations or providing feed back to the supervisors on their performance involving interaction with the workforce -- their key responsibility! I have had many useful discussions with groups of supervisors using this model. In the course of these, a number of them candidly shared with me information that included such jewels of insight as the fact that they were uncomfortable confronting workers, some of whom were long-time friends.

ACCOUNTABILITY

61. ACCOUNTABILITY IS THE SIGN OF A HEALTHY ORGANIZATION

Accountability should therefore also be routinely observed.

A vital element of any organization involves the degree to which employees, both working level and management, feel compelled to do the best they can at their jobs. With some individuals, this compulsion is natural and comes from within themselves. With others, it is something that must be fostered by the organization. This fostering is best done through establishment of a strong sense of accountability.

Those wishing to avoid confrontation will want to fog any discussion of accountability, and at the mention of it, will go off on academic discussions of supposedly revolutionary techniques such as "positive accountability," wherein management action is restricted to positive reinforcement. It is usually this same contingent that denigrates the concept of accountability by equating it to punishment or disciplinary action and consequently views accountability as only a negative force.

I have had this reaction so frequently that I avoid use of the term "accountability" when working with some organizations, and speak instead of "consequences." Accountability is, after all, nothing more than consequences for one's actions. It is what exists when those who fall short in expected performance feel badly that they have not carried out their function as they are compensated for doing. Experience indicates that it is also the first characteristic that must be instilled in those organizations that require a significant positive change in performance (sometimes referred to as "turn-around" situations).

What does a lack of accountability look like? It looks like long overdue corrective actions; it looks like lack of challenges in meetings when someone does not deliver on his part of the effort. It looks like no "heat" felt in interactions when someone does not deliver on a commitment made; it looks like workers knowing but not acting like they know management's expectations, without a sense that someone will question them on it or that there will be a consequence to their actions.

A good observer needs to be alert for the many excuses out there for not holding people accountable. One I have heard more times than I care to count involves the sympathy factor. For example, one manager once told me, "It's very hard to hold people accountable for not getting things done because we don't have enough resources." This manager was surrendering before the battle even began. If he did not have the resources he truly needed, he should have gotten them. If he couldn't get them, for whatever reason, he should have fought the battle with whatever weapon was available, such as a push for greater efficiency, extended work hours, or other productivity improving techniques. As a side note, I have been amazed on a number of occasions at how quickly the issue of lack of resources sheds its costume and leaves the area when accountability in an organization is strengthened.

For an observer's purpose, two red flags can call attention to shortfalls in accountability within an organization:

1.   The message from management that admits to significant problems, but at the same time complements or applauds everyone in the work force.

61a. *BE SKEPTICAL OF THE CONCLUSION THAT "THINGS ARE ALL SCREWED UP BUT EVERYBODY IS DOING A GREAT JOB"*

2.   The other is "happy talk"

61b. *BE ALERT FOR HAPPY TALK -- PARTICULARLY IN MEETINGS*

The degree of accountability can be observed by sitting in on several meetings where performance of the organization is discussed. Be alert in these meetings for "happy talk." This is the kind of talk that is enjoyable to those not actively engaged in ensuring their organization is among the best performers. It comes from an unfounded belief that everything is OK; there are no major problems; those few minor problems that may exist are understood and well on their way to being resolved. It is the kind of talk that brings comfort to those unwilling to confront others. It is also the kind of talk that is misleading and that does little to move an organization ahead.

Observing accountability is one of those activities in which the exposure referred to in AACT 2 comes heavily into play. What does accountability look like in a well run organization? Among other things in such a place, there are accountability-oriented meetings, where performance in terms of results is discussed, and people are held accountable for having done what they said they were going to do. There is an atmosphere that the workforce is not a "family" where members are tolerated and loved no matter what they do, but rather a "team" where people support each other but every player is expected to carry his share of the load. Those who fall short are told so in no uncertain terms. One method that has been used successfully by a number of organizations to exercise accountability while dealing fairly and effectively with bargaining unit personnel is the MARC process. This process was developed by Management Associated Results Company, Inc. located in Terre Haute, Indiana. The MARC method uses fundamental management techniques such as early coaching, providing candid feedback, and documenting performance. Although not intended as such, it can serve as a primer for exercising accountability that applies equally well to other than bargaining unit situations.

COMPLACENCY

Observing how well an organization learns from others provides a measure of a potentially fatal organizational disease -- complacency.

62. *COMPLACENCY IS MOST EVIDENT IN THE LACK OF LEARNING FROM OTHERS*

Complacency is that cancer of organizations that inhibits people from acknowledging their weak points and allows them to live in a baseless euphoria that they are really good. It is an illness propagated by ignorance of how much better others are, even if only in limited areas. It is an illness that makes it worth the effort to observe for it. To observe whether or not it exists, ask a few people, at various levels, what other organizations they have visited recently in order to learn from the experiences of others. Be sure to ask, not what they learned, but <u>what they actually put into practice as a result</u> of what they learned. Those afflicted with complacency will tell you either they have not visited others, or, as a number of individuals have told me when asked, they looked at other places and "all we learned was that we do things better than they do." This response is, in itself, a red flag that complacency is setting in. A good observer will rigorously pursue to what degree an organization being observed is learning from others. This includes verifying that responses to questions in this area are supportable with concrete information.

Organizations that are complacent also have a tendency to selectively listen to only news that fortifies what they already believe, that is, that they are good. These are organizations that should but do not have in place the concept of,

63. *BELIEVE YOUR WORST INDICATION*

This is one of those simple rules that was branded on my mind and proven to be valid time and again in my years operating nuclear submarines. It serves well in providing a simple but conservative approach to operating in an environment where below-par performance is intolerable. In the most straightforward example, suppose one were pressurizing a tank and observing two pressure gauges. Suppose one gauge indicated the pressure was beyond the maximum to which the tank could be pressurized before it burst, while the other one indicated pressure was considerably below the limit and everything was OK. Which indication would you believe? A submariner would believe his worst indication and act accordingly; in this case immediately reducing pressure. You probably would also, if you appreciated the potential consequences that might be imminent. This conservative approach is also a sound one to be followed in the management arena, where the consequences of a wrong decision may not at first appear to be as drastic or as imminent. I can't count the number of times that after briefing an executive on problems I had found in the performance of his employees, the executive responded by challenging me, because, "another oversight group just looked at that area and said everything was fine." Depending on the circumstances, one could debate until the fires of hell cool, which of these reports provides the indicator that is most accurate. Be certain, however, that history has shown numerous times that it is better to act on a problem you might not have than not to act on one that you do. It is also usually the case that those who prefer to believe their best indication are the same ones who enjoy getting good news and who sometimes unknowingly send that message to their employees.

THE NEW-GUY SYNDROME

Half-life is a concept used both in physics and in biology. It is essentially the time that elapses before some number of any items is reduced by half. It was developed to describe the reduction in the number of particular nuclei resulting from radioactive decay and/or the decline in ingested material resulting from biological elimination. The term can, however, be applied to managers, the reduction of which comes from firing, transfer, or other departure reasons. A long half-life for managers reflects a stable situation, in which management turnover is at a minimum. This short treatise on half-life is provided only to ensure an understanding of my comment that the half-life of managers in high-pressure situations is often quite short. Consequently, an observer in any but the most low-key professional fields will frequently interface with a manager new to either his position, to the organization, or to both. The caution to the observer in interacting with this type of manager is,

64. *BEWARE OF THE NEW GUY TELLING YOU EVERYTHING IS BROKEN*

On occasion, you may find that the new guy is right, and it would be negligent on the observer's part not to follow-up on such allegations. However, the operative word here is follow-up, so that any conclusions drawn are conclusions of the observer based on objective information. Keep in mind that a new individual will, by his human nature, tend to look at what is facing him as being at the bottom of the pit. Why wouldn't he? If he admits that something is good, and if it is later found to be less than good, then the finger points straight at him. On the other hand, if he convinces the right people that everything is screwed up when he comes in, he can't lose. If it's screwed up later, he can always say it was even more screwed up than he thought. If he makes any improvements, slight as they may be, they will have to be viewed as progress since he's already defined the condition that everything was screwed up when he got here.

THE USE OF PROBLEMS

In examining management issues, the observer needs to know that "ghost" management problems are easy to find. These are the kinds of problems that don't really exist. If they appear at all, it is only in one's mind. I can see one of these ghosts by observing that you, as a manager, are not doing some things the way I, and possibly others, think they should be done. As a result, I conclude that you have a management problem. I may be absolutely convinced this ghost is real. You as a manager may be doing something completely unorthodox. You may never get out into the work spaces. You may have no use for performance indicators. You may not set goals. You may be a tyrant with employees. Those, other than the naïve, will recognize, as discussed earlier, that there are many ways of managing, any one of which can be successful. To keep this in mind, the management observer needs to apply the concept that,

65. IF YOU DON'T HAVE A PERFORMANCE PROBLEM, YOU DON'T HAVE A MANAGEMENT PROBLEM

This concept is similar to AACT 9 [SO WHAT?] but when management problems are involved, the issue is more complex. The performance problems that are the results of management problems are not always clearly linked to those management problems. Consequently, AACT 9 may not work in these cases. On the other hand, considerable observer time can be saved by first looking for performance problems. Should those be found, pursuit of what the contributing management problems might be is a useful one. But if performance problems are not found, one can safely assume that management problems don't exist. In other words, don't go into an apple picking business and first focus on why the apple pickers' boss does not use some management techniques that you think he should, such as walking around the orchard. First go to the orchard and find out if the apples are being picked properly, safely, and efficiently. If they are, leave the orchard and let the apple-picking business continue with the purpose of its existence.

The management observer is well advised to examine the recurrence, if any, of the various key performance problems in an organization. This can be done with a single sheet of paper on which you list a cursory description of each problem and its general time frame. These might be extracted from internal or external oversight reports, coupled with the observer's own view of current performance. This problem matrix can be a very telling piece of work, because,

66. *A PROBLEM MATRIX IS A SELF-PORTRAIT OF THE EFFECTIVENESS OF THE MANAGEMENT TEAM*

The matrix can be constructed by listing the general categories of any problems that currently exist at the facility on the ordinate or y axis, and the time frame of identification of this or similar problems on the abscissa. The time frame can be determined either from reports describing the problem or from discussions with various managers. The depiction that can be constructed allows longstanding or recurring problems to be easily identified. Of course, since managers are paid to fix problems, the recurrence of problems is a measure of management effectiveness. It is also, in a sense, a portrait of how effective the management team is -- a portrait they have painted themselves. This depiction of recurring problems also lays the groundwork for some informative discussion with the managers as to why these problems are so difficult to resolve.

The above exercise is one example of a concept that is useful not only to the observer, but also to the observed organization.

67. *OBSERVERS PROVIDE A MIRROR FOR MANAGERS*

Managers and supervisors, just like every other human being, are sometimes unaware of that little spot of barbeque sauce on their face or that little blemish in their performance, or the sloppy habits that they've settled into over time -- until they look into a mirror. An observer providing an observation report is providing that mirror. I have often found it useful to go out in a facility, observe what managers do and the conditions they either cause or tolerate, and then have an open group discussion with the managers to show them how they are perceived by others from outside their organization. At one facility, the management team was quite confident they had a handle on all of their performance shortfalls and were equally confident they had actions in place to correct them. Their confidence was strongly based on their assumption that they had few problems anyway because they were really good. Upon my arrival at the facility I went directly into the workplace and observed some points to the contrary. The following are examples:

- A sensitive and potentially hazardous evolution was in progress. Precise face to face communications, which were the industry norm, were essential in this evolution to ensure effective transfer of information and close control of the activities. The manager in charge of the evolution, when he received a critical report on the position of an important piece of equipment, gave no verbal response but rather responded with a "thumbs up" gesture. Another manager, who later arrived to relieve the person in charge of the evolution, bellowed across the room upon his entry, to the person he would relieve, "Is it still perking?" The response was "Yeah." This was the extent of the information exchanged between the oncoming and off-going manager, and the transfer of responsibilities was consummated.

• I observed an improperly operating piece of facility equipment, and pointed it out to several operators, supervisors, and a manager. Although everyone to whom I mentioned the malfunctioning component took it seriously and immediately began trying to figure out what was wrong, no one even considered getting out the operating manual provided with the equipment, which was required by facility policy to be used when operating the component. I brought this to the attention of the man in charge when he was about to give direction to operate the item in a manner prohibited by the manual -- which I was standing there reading!

• I passed by a safety inspector who was in the process of telling a supervisor that the area in which his electricians were working on energized electrical equipment needed to have a safety tape barrier. The barrier would prevent others not engaged in the work from coming in contact with the high voltage equipment. The supervisor responded to the inspector's comment with the counterchallenge, "Prove it." Being unable to expeditiously identify the source of the directive, the safety inspector left and the condition remained unchanged (until some several hours later when the document containing the requirement for safety barriers was located).

These observations provided excellent fuel for a burning dialogue with the management team. I sculpted the discussion around an objective which I posed as a question to the management team: Determine why these things were happening in a facility where the managers firmly believed they were doing a really good job. The discussion coupled with the undeniable facts of the observation allowed the managers to see themselves in an objective if not complimentary light. Because I departed the facility shortly thereafter I can only hope that the discussion caused them to be a little less confident and perhaps more critical in looking at themselves in the future.

THE VALUE OF "SOFT" INFORMATION

As with all information developed in the course of observation activities, it is most useful when this information is objective, verifiable, and based on hard evidence. It is this basis that allows the observer to convey the information in a compelling way. However, there is another category of information that can be just as useful, but is developed using the kinesthetics of one's mind. Kinesthesia is that ability that allows an archer shooting instinctively to know where to hold his bow before releasing an arrow at a target at which he is not technically "aiming." In laymen's terms it can also be described as just "knowing what to do." When a person has been in a field for forty to fifty years, she develops a set of instincts that are based on her numerous experiences, even though in many cases she may not even be able to recall the specific experiences. It is this phenomena that allows an experienced individual to look at something briefly and just know it is wrong, without being able to explain why or to justify her conclusion. So,

68. *PAY ATTENTION TO THE GUT FEELINGS OF EXPERIENCED PEOPLE*

I use myself as an example here only to personalize my point. I have had the opportunity to work with many individuals much more capable in forming quick and accurate conclusions than I am. That said, because of the breadth of my experience, I feel confident that I can come into a facility, observe a few activities, talk to a few managers, and relying on my gut feelings, form a reasonably accurate conclusion regarding the organization's performance and some of the key strengths and problem areas. What I'm really doing is positioning pieces of a puzzle and visualizing the entire picture with the missing pieces temporarily filled in by drawing on my experience with multitudes of other organizations. I can observe one minor indication of a performance problem, and just "know" that the other symptoms of that problem will be there when I look for them. This allows me to come to quicker conclusions than a person with less experience. These "gut' feelings" are particularly valuable because they are a reasonably accurate product developed without a full expenditure of time and effort. They can be even more valuable because they are in the realm of "feelings" rather than that of concrete, observable, measurable information. This allows them to capture underlying performance issues that most oversight organizations would never even consider getting into, such as, the sense of urgency, internalization of principles, and ownership of issues. Highly effective leaders of operating facilities, when given the opportunity to interact with experienced people who have just observed their facility will take advantage of this opportunity by probing these "gut feelings." The request by the facility leader goes something like this: "Don't worry about whether or not you have specific examples or bases for your conclusions. Tell me your impressions and your gut feelings about this place." Highly effective observers given the same opportunity will do likewise.

CULTURE

Much has been written in various management tomes about "culture," to the point that the term "culture" has taken on a life of its own. It is the bread upon which uncountable numbers of consultants subsist. As I write this, "culture surveys" are in vogue. If you want to make your organization better and you don't know what to do, have a culture survey done, or at least that is what some would say -- but not me. I believe that the world of performance is all about behavior. A behavior that exists can be observed, and conversely, if a behavior cannot be observed it does not exist. Some may argue that culture can be observed, but if so, why are these currently popular culture surveys primarily constructed from interviews and not observations? That is enough criticizing of the term "culture." I can accept use of the term and I can fit it into my set of beliefs based on experience in the field of organizational performance. My point in making small of it is only to emphasize that there is value in keeping things simple, and one of the things that is most valuable if kept simple is terminology. Culture is, by definition in The American Heritage Dictionary of the English Language, "The totality of socially transmitted behavior patterns, arts, beliefs, institutions, and all other products of human work and thought characteristic of a community or population." Can you imagine yourself directing one of your observers, be they a direct report manager or an oversight person, to "Go out in the facility and observe the totality of socially transmitted behavior patterns, arts, beliefs, institutions, and all other products of human work and thought"? Or might it be more useful to direct the person to, "Go out in the facility and tell me how people are behaving and your insights on why they are behaving that way? For these reasons I encourage avoiding the faddish term, culture, and sticking with more basic terms.

With the above as a lead-in, I offer the following advice on how to observe the role (if any) that safety plays in the operation of organizations, particularly in high hazard industries such as chemical, nuclear, and healthcare -- what in today's terms is often referred to as "safety culture." I observed safety culture for decades before I had ever heard of the term culture. To do so, I simply looked to see how behaviors in an organization compared with those to which I had become accustomed in the nuclear submarine force, where the importance of nuclear safety was clearly evident and well reflected in its safety record. Over time, without giving terminology much thought other than maintaining my fundamental principle of always trying to keep communications simple, I came to using the approach of pursuing the following questions: What level of attention is placed on safety? How important does the organization consider safety to be? Where in the priorities of a company does safety fall? Rather than accept verbal answers to these questions, I looked for observable behaviors that would more likely tell the truth. I also came to understand that within industries that have a potential for hazard, and there are many of these, attention to or a focus on safety was synonymous with a focus on good operation. Thus the concept,

69. *YOU CAN'T HAVE A FOCUS ON GOOD OPERATION WITHOUT HAVING A FOCUS ON SAFETY*

Much has been written about safety focus, and it is likely that at least being among the first to address the topic was the International Atomic Energy Agency (IAEA) in Vienna.

Although the IAEA writings on the subject deal with nuclear safety focus, the principles can well apply to safety in other arenas as well. For example, the principles of patient safety in the healthcare arena are not unlike those of nuclear safety. Regardless of what field of work one is discussing, the concept of a safety focus, even if limited to maintaining a safe environment for employees and or clients, is a most important one. There is a strong albeit subjective correlation between an organization's attention to safety and its general adherence to high standards in all areas. Unfortunately, many of the writings available on safety focus provide little practical information on how to effectively observe this important area.

The objective of any observation of safety focus should be to determine if the organization has sufficiently engrained the importance of safety into everyone in the organization. If this is so, then safety will not only be seen as (and believed by employees to be) a priority of executive management, but will be <u>demonstrated by the actions</u> of all employees, <u>evident by its presence</u> in all environments, and <u>strongly considered during key decision making</u>.

Insight into the degree of safety focus of an organization can be gained by observing the following:

1. **Does the behavior of employees reflect a strong safety focus?**
   If safety focus is strong, this will be reflected in workers placing high priority on complying not only with practices that would preclude imminent and extreme harm, but also practices that would reduce the likelihood of <u>any</u> harm. For example, in the healthcare arena, caregivers not closely adhering to policies governing hand cleansing to prevent infection, or the proper identification of patients

before treatment, reflect a less-than-strong focus on patient safety.

2. **Is there an <u>evident</u> presence of safety focus in the work environment?**
    This presence might be evident in signs and postings, minutes of meetings, records of senior management discussions with the workforce, in criteria for employee performance appraisals, and most importantly, in the day-to-day discussions of employees and particularly managers. A good positive example is the fact that at most nuclear power plants in the United States, every routine daily meeting typically starts with either a comment or short discussion on safety -- every meeting.

3. **Is there a strong safety focus message from management?**
    This includes a clear and direct message from the highest levels of management, relayed and regularly enforced by the various management and supervisory levels, that safety is a top priority. This message would be communicated in such a way that employees understand what that message means to them and what kind of behaviors they are expected to exhibit in order to meet management's expectations on this point. A useful way to get additional insight in this area is to ask the front-line employees what the top focus of management is, or ask new employees what key message they can recall from their new employee training and orientation. Ask them what this message means to them. Most importantly, what do they <u>do differently</u> in their day-to-day work that they would not do if it were not for this message?

4. **Is safety routinely considered when key management decisions are made?**

All businesses are under some amount of economic pressure. Given that this pressure is there, when difficult decisions need to be made, it should be apparent that any impact on safety has been taken into consideration in making those decisions. The key word in the previous sentence is "apparent." Not only should the impact on safety be considered, but it should be <u>apparent to employees</u> that management has considered the safety implications of difficult economic decisions. This in itself is a strong message to all that safety is important. For the observer, it can be useful to discuss with managers difficult economic decisions that had to be made recently, such as a downsizing, and ask specifically how they took the impact of that decision on safety into account. Were any compensating measures put in place? It can also be helpful to ask the employees if the managers have "walked the talk" -- can the employees discuss any examples of management making difficult decisions with a clear and evident priority placed on safety? Have the employees at least had explained to them how safety was taken into consideration when making such decisions?

THE CORPORATE FUNCTION

Even in the structurally changing organizations of today, it is difficult if not impossible to effectively observe management without probing into the corporate function. As a matter of fact, it could be argued that if the corporate function is not worth observing, it is not worth having. One of the first questions to be asked in assessing the corporate function is, what is the role of the corporate office? In the plainest terms, if a corporate function exists, then,

70. *CORPORATE EXISTS FOR A PRIMARY REASON -- TO PROVIDE SUPPORT AND OVERSIGHT OF THE OPERATING FACILITIES*

I recall the CEO of one large organization reinforcing this to the corporate staff by first showing the direct link between the performance of the production facilities, where operations are conducted, and the company's financial bottom line. His emphasis was on operations. He then reminded the corporate staff that the only things operated at the corporate office are the knobs on the office doors. This was a strong reinforcement of his expectation that the value of the operating facilities was expected to be recognized, and the focus of the corporate staff was to be on supporting those facilities and their operation.

Recognizing and accepting this fact makes it relatively easy to observe the corporate function. However, the corporate observation does not begin at, nor can it be done solely at, the corporate office. It begins where the reason for being is, that is, at the working facility-- factory, plant, store, hospital, or other facility.

Typical corporate oversight consists of morning phone calls between the corporate and the facility staffs, a set of performance indicators, usually updated monthly, and occasional VIP-type visits by senior management to well-groomed-in-advance areas of the facility. In a word, this is inadequate. Having led numerous observations of large corporate organizations, I quickly developed a pattern that always bore fruit in terms of useful information for the company. As an observer, visit the working area, and find out what is going on, using the techniques and concepts discussed herein. The result of this review should be concentrated on developing a list of the top two or three problems in each of several functional areas, as well as the top problems in the management area. Recognize that these "problems" need not even be recognized as such by the staff at the operating facility. In fact, if they are not, that is a valuable piece of information in itself. Along with identifying these problems the observer should develop an understanding of the actions being taken to solve them (for the cases where the problems are recognized by the facility staff). It is always a fruitful question to ask the various levels at the working facility: If you were king, and could have or do anything you want, what would you do to solve this problem? Equipped with the above information, the observer can unfortunately rest assured that he likely now knows more about that company than the vast majority of people at the corporate office. The remaining question then becomes: If the corporate staff doesn't know what the problems of the facility are, what does that say for their oversight role, and how can they possibly provide support if they don't know what support is needed?

The issue of accountability discussed earlier is just as important at the corporate level as it is at the operating facility. So the following is a good line of questioning to pursue: Is the corporate staff held accountable for facility performance in their areas -- for example, would the corporate oversight manager be held accountable if a regulatory oversight body found the recurrence of a regulatory problem at the operating facility? How is performance in each of the functional areas at the facility reflected in the compensation of the corporate counterparts for those areas?

CHAPTER 7
WHAT TO DO WITH YOUR INFORMATION

The product of an observer's activities is information, whether that observer is doing a formal assessment or executing her responsibilities as a line manager. For that information to serve a purpose it will need to be communicated. That communication is what this chapter is about and is at least as important as any of the information-gathering material discussed so far. Regardless of the potential value of information collected, if it is not communicated in the most effective way, that potential will not be fully tapped. I have experienced uncountable numbers of would be observers who diligently and with considerable expertise collected information, only to fail in the end because they were unable to effectively transfer this information to those who would act on it.

This chapter can be useful to the observer tasked with developing a written report of the performance of an organization. However, the concepts and techniques discussed herein also can be helpful to anyone communicating a message to others.

PROCESSING THE INFORMATION COLLECTED

How does one process all of the information collected in an observation? As discussed in AACTS 12 and 21, if you [IGNORE THE GRAY INFORMATION] and [WRITE DOWN EVERYTHING], you will be well on your way to providing a valuable message. You already have its content. The next step is to craft it into an instrument of change, a document of such interest that people will not be able to put it down once they begin reading it, a document or verbal report that will compel the receiver to take action.

Early in the observation process, start transcribing your very rough notes (I assume they will be very rough since hopefully you spent more effort on watching activities and listening to what each person was telling you rather than on making note of one particular thing you saw or the last thing some person said.) In transcribing the notes, carve them into meaningful statements that can be used to tell a story. For example, you may have scribbled down, "supervisor – O/T -- no idea." Later you might transcribe this personal shorthand into "The responsible supervisor, when questioned about how much overtime his direct reports use, said he had "no idea." Specific quotes of others typically carry more weight than your words and can be used to provide perspective in debriefing senior management. In the above example, "no idea" makes it evident that this was not a simple case of a supervisor understanding the amount of overtime worked but being off by a few hours. Rather it indicates that he was apparently totally disconnected from what his direct reports are doing relative to use of overtime. As another example, you may have noted "N entered rm. – 3 sec.—no soap." This might be transcribed as, "The nurse rinsed her hands for only 3 seconds, without using soap, prior to entering the patient's room. This is contrary to hospital policy that requires either use of a sanitizing gel or washing the hands for 15 seconds using the antibacterial soap provided at each washing station." If the observer transcribes this note within a short time after the observation, additional information not initially recorded may also come to mind, such as, "The nurse commented that finding the sanitizing gel container at the room entrance empty happens frequently and is frustrating to the nurses." This could be a useful part of the observation because it provides a string to be pulled regarding the maintenance of hand cleansing agents.

USE OF EXAMPLES

Examples are the "pictures" of the written word. You likely will remember an old Chinese proverb: "A picture is worth a thousand words." If you do, your recollection would not be correct. That statement is a misinterpretation of the original proverb, which actually stated: "A picture's meaning can express ten thousand words," the latter interpretation providing a better balance between the value of pictures and words. But as stated either way, the proverb provides a powerful analogy that can be applied to both the written and spoken word. For simplicity we'll use the less accurate but more concise form:

71. *AN EXAMPLE IS WORTH A THOUSAND WORDS*

Apply this AACT and use examples, whether you are writing an observation report, or trying to make a compelling point to your boss. Use a lot of examples, and use graphic examples. By "graphic," I mean examples that paint a vivid picture of whatever point it is that you are making. To say that workers were not well coordinated in what they were trying to do is one thing. To describe how one group of workers showed up to disassemble a piece of equipment at the same time that another group showed up to operate the equipment for a test, paints a visual picture of a Keystone Cops-like scenario and puts meaning behind the words. It includes a sense of the importance of the point, as well as makes it easier to understand, digest, and remember. I can't count the number of times, in follow-up discussions with managers, months after I performed observations for them, the only things they remembered about my final brief were the graphic examples I had used.

How many examples one should use is a function of the circumstances under which they are being used. In a written report, the tone of the report needs to be considered as well as the length. More examples tend to make the tone of a written report harsher. In the case of verbal reports, the presentation should be adapted to the specific audience, with the presenter continuously staying in tune with the body language of the receiver. If, in describing a point to an executive, his facial expressions indicate he understands the point after the first example, then stop. To drone on with the other examples would be rude as well as a waste of his time. The question of how many examples one should have at his fingertips is a different point. A good guide in this regard is the number three. When you intend to make an important point, it is useful to have at least three well thought out and descriptive examples at the ready. One meaningful example is typically all that is needed to convey a point. However, there is always a possibility that some aspect of an example will not be quite accurate. In this case, the presenter stands to lose credibility. Having at least three examples at the ready allows for at least one to be discounted, one to be used, and one to be held as a backup in the event the receiver wants to hear more. This rule of three examples has never failed me

Transcribe the individual notes you have taken during any assessment activity into separate categories, based on what your gut feelings tell you the issues may be. These will form your hypotheses. For example, the category into which an example might fall could be "supervisory awareness." The hypothesis might be: "Most supervisors are unaware of the most frequently occurring performance shortfalls of their workers." Don't worry much about the hypotheses selected. These will define themselves as the process continues. Should one hypothesis not have much basis to support it near the conclusion of the note compilation, it is a safe bet that the hypothesis was incorrect. If the incremental information collected but not falling under a strongly supported hypothesis still might be useful to senior management, it can be relayed to them as separate but important information. If not, just drop it. In those cases where the hypothesis is valid, the supporting information can be used to put it in perspective, and to weave a story that will be useful in convincing the receiving manager that action needs to be taken. Obviously, a lap-top computer can be a useful tool in this exercise.

BALANCE AND PRIORITIZATION IN THE MESSAGE

I have often heard, usually from the lower levels of the receiving organization, that reports need to be "balanced," that is, the bad points balanced with good points. I would say that reports should be accurate and that if anything is to be balanced, it should be the performance of the organization that should be balanced, and it should be balanced by those responsible for performance. When problems exist, those in charge should push even harder for good performance to offset these negative aspects of performance. Having said this, I would caution the aggressive observer to,

72. *MAKE NOTE OF POSITIVES*

Aspects of an organization that are truly and outstandingly positive should be noted and communicated as such. The emphasis here is on "outstandingly." It shouldn't be necessary to look for positives of this caliber; they should stand out. If the goal of observation is improvement, as it is, it will not be a good use of observer time to document all of the numerous positive aspects that are apparent in most organizations. In the course of observing the various aspects of an organization the most striking positives will be apparent. The collection of positives will speak for itself. If nothing stands out as impressive, then write nothing down. If the thoroughness of some program or procedure is impressive, write that down. At the end of the review, if the only positive thing that strikes you is the quality of some document, that in itself tells you (and management) something -- they have few positive aspects that differentiate them from every other organization and therefore are likely to be either mediocre or to have significant problems.

As a caveat to the above, the aggressive observer needs to be sensitive to the fact that he or she will at one time or another fall into the negativity rut. It is natural for one so focused on finding things that are problems to begin to see everything from a negative perspective. This doesn't mean that you should go off and waste your time searching for "good" things just so you can make some receivers happier. Far from it. But one should be alert to recognize when negativity may be creeping in to everything the observer sees and says. Periodically stand back and ask yourself, "Are things really that bad here?" When I have used this self-examination exercise on a number of occasions, especially after identifying a relatively large number of problems at a facility, my answer to myself was sometimes, "No things are not that bad. This place is well run, but there are a number of problems that indicate considerable opportunity to get even better." This response helped me to put myself in the proper frame of mind, achieve the right tone in the delivery of my findings, and protect the credibility of the effort.

In every assessment that is properly done, it will be necessary for the observer to do what is most difficult for a dedicated observer -- disregard some of her information. This is based on the premise that she will have collected a tremendous amount of information, and will be delivering it to managers or executives who have neither the time nor the inclination to listen to every morsel of information collected. Consequently, it is essential that one,

73. *PRIORITIZE YOUR KEY POINTS AND KEEP THEM TO A FEW*

This is particularly true for executive level briefings, but is also useful in developing summaries of reports that are often the only part of reports that are read.

Prioritizing points is an easy exercise, although one used not nearly often enough by observers. On a flip chart or white board, or even a blank piece of paper, concisely list all of the key points of your conclusions. Then prioritize them, getting inputs from any others who may have helped in developing the conclusions. Number the points in descending priority, using your own judgment combined with the judgment of your colleagues -- if you're fortunate enough to not be flying solo in the observation. Disregard all greater than three or four at most, and you will have a powerful message to deliver to your customer.

THE   IMPORTANCE   OF   BEING   CONCISE, COMPELLING, AND FACTUAL

I have known an uncountable number of observers in my professional life, at all levels from entry to the executive level. Many of these were among the best in collecting information; however, as observers, many failed -- primarily because they were unable to effectively communicate their information. The operative word here is "effectively." Don't take this section lightly, thinking it is obvious that communicating effectively is important and I and everyone else know that. There is more to the point in assessment space. For observation information to be effectively communicated means it must be transmitted in a way that causes action to be taken to address the issues communicated. Remember,

74. *THE MISSION OF AN OBSERVER IS NOT ONLY TO FIND PROBLEMS, IT IS TO PRECIPITATE POSITIVE CHANGE*

To achieve this, the assessor must,

75. *TELL A COMPELLING STORY*

I could list hundreds of examples where this part of the process broke down, and the value of the observations melted like a snow cone in a Phoenix summer. Many of these examples involve senior executives performing in oversight roles. Typically these executives would average about 40 years of experience at senior levels and consequently had tremendous insight. These are the kinds of people I was talking about when I discussed AACT 68 [PAY ATTENTION TO THE GUT FEELINGS OF EXPERIENCED PEOPLE.] But many of these executives, when placed in an observation role, believed they were "too senior" to perform the menial task of writing a set of notes, to organize their thoughts, to "stir the tea leaves," or to apply many of the concepts and techniques discussed above.

The intuition of these executives, particularly in observations of corporate activities, was impressive as they processed what they saw and heard through a mental data bank built up over decades of experience. But as observers on their own, they were frequently of limited use. Why? Because they didn't have the detailed information collected, sorted, and analyzed in a way that would allow them to relay their impressions and conclusions in a compelling way. I recall one such executive team member who after spending less than a half day at a visited organization came to me as the team leader for a corporate observation and said, "I'm done and I'm leaving. This place is all screwed up." He then left. As it turns out, he was absolutely right; but the value he added to the team and to the organization being observed was zero.

What does compelling sound like? It sounds like something that when heard results in an immediate urge to do something about it; to fix it. Compelling is something that you cannot ignore. I once had an observation team member witness a briefing of workers by a supervisor. The intent of the briefing was to ensure that the workers understood the job to which they had been assigned, and were aware of the safety precautions associated with the work. The observer noted correctly that the supervisor's briefing was terse and overly general regarding personnel safety. The supervisor's cautions were limited to the direction, "Be careful when you're working near the valve." (The work was on a large valve that could automatically actuate, causing the guillotine-like dropping of a large metal arm.) The observer intended to communicate this to the manager of the facility as an example of the need for supervisors to perform more thorough pre-job briefings. The specific words he intended to use were,

"We observed a supervisor's pre-job briefing in which detailed safety precautions were not reviewed with the workers."

I jumped on the opportunity to coach the well-intentioned observer. Through a combination of combing through the observer's notes, asking the workers and supervisor several follow-up questions, pulling the string, and going out into the workplace to observe the valve on which the work was to be performed, we acquired some additional information. The intended briefing was revised to include the following points:

- The supervisor's review of safety precautions was limited to "be careful."

- The guillotine-like arm of the large valve could drop unexpectedly while the workers were near it. The work at one point required a worker to have his hand and possibly his head under the large metal arm.

- An accident had occurred during this same work on this valve two years ago when the valve arm dropped and a worker lost a finger. This case was still in litigation.

- One of the commitments of the company to a regulator, as a result of the previous accident, was to improve the quality of pre-job safety briefs.

Which would better motivate you to take corrective action: The points listed above, or a mundane statement that a pre-job brief didn't cover specific safety precautions? That is what compelling is.

It is worth noting here that the attribute which can be either most helpful or most detrimental to the compelling nature of a statement or story is "perspective", that is, how deep is the water (how significant is the issue); how wide is the pool (how broad is the issue)?

An issue identified in a healthcare setting may be based on having observed only one example (a narrow pool), provided the depth of the water is significant. For instance, if the example observed resulted in the near death of a patient, the issue would clearly be significant and warrant management attention. A different issue may be considerably less significant by itself, such as an anesthetist having a syringe on his cart that is informally and not very clearly labeled. However, if the pool is quite wide in that none out of a large number of anesthetist's syringes observed were properly labeled, considering that administration of the wrong drug by injection during anesthesia is a too frequently occurring event in healthcare, the issue may also be of significance.

The most common weakness of observers regarding the use of perspective is not including it in describing their issue or observation. Don't be guilty of this shortfall. Check yourself to ensure you have described how deep is the water; how wide is the pool.

The message conveyed to the customer in an assessment activity needs not only be compelling, it needs to be simple and concise. I have concluded after working with numerous observers (and many line managers who reported to me as well) that,

76. *IF YOU CAN'T DESCRIBE A PROBLEM IN ONE OR TWO SIMPLE SENTENCES, YOU DON'T UNDERSTAND THE PROBLEM.*

While an object, like a problem, a condition, or any observation, is in our mind, we tend to see it as oversimplified. The mind forms a mental picture of the object, and without our realizing it, draws on hundreds of bits of information to clarify that picture. It is not until we try to transform that picture into written words that we find how complex the picture really is. For example, think of the simple picture of a small metal bolt with a nut on the end of it. That's easy to picture in your mind, isn't it? Now take a piece of paper and write down a description of that object which will allow another person who has never seen a nut or bolt to form a mental picture identical to yours. Not so easy, huh? Now think how much more complicated this gets when the picture has multiple objects in it and they are moving and talking as they do in many problem descriptions. The take away on this point is, don't be confident that you understand a problem and how to communicate it until you've put it in writing. Even if you're preparing a verbal report, try putting it in writing first. You may find that you don't have enough information to accurately and concisely make the report. You may find you don't really understand the problem. If you can't describe it concisely, you don't.

A common barrier in communication between an observer and his customer, particularly when that customer is at the senior levels of management, is the use of jargon. You may be able to describe a problem concisely using jargon familiar to you, but what do you do when the jargon is like Greek to a non-Greek speaking customer? Assessment results are typically delivered to managers at such a level in the organization that they no longer have the time to remain current on the technical details and jargon of any field. These people similarly have little time to waste trying to translate and interpret issues described to them in other than clear and concise language.

In preparing for a presentation or in developing a report, try describing the problem as you would if you were telling it to an old friend that you just ran into -- an old friend who is working in a completely different field from yours. I refer to this as "street terms," and I can't count the numbers of times my first response on hearing an observer's identified problem was "tell me the problem in street terms." You can easily imagine some highly intelligent technician describing a problem in a very compelling way to another highly intelligent technician in the same field, and being very effective in communicating the issue using commonly understood jargon. But how do you concisely describe venous thromboembolism to a nuclear engineer, or neutron flux oscillations in a boiling water reactor to a nurse? It can be done and it can be done well. It just takes effort and a thorough understanding of the problem to achieve the simplicity needed for the message to have effect. As a side note, be advised that meanings for the same terms which differ between fields of expertise further complicate communications. I recall a person from a nuclear plant describing to a group of healthcare professionals how supervisors are conceptually like the third leg of a stool, in that they provide a fundamental part of a steady management foundation. The audience found the analogy amusing as they tried to picture a "stool" (in the medical context of body waste) having three legs.

Once you have achieved an adequate level of conciseness, an acid test that can be used to judge whether or not your description of a problem is adequate, is to see if the question, So What? would be a logical one following your statement of the problem. (This question and its purpose was described in AACT 9, but here is used for a different but equally useful purpose.) If it would be logical to ask this question, you have not described the problem well enough. If in describing it you find yourself reverting to writing a long paragraph, or worse yet, several paragraphs, go back to AACT 76 [IF YOU CAN'T DESCRIBE A PROBLEM IN ONE OR TWO SIMPLE SENTENCES, YOU DON'T UNDERSTAND THE PROBLEM.]

In separating and analyzing the information you have collected in your notes during an assessment activity,

77. SEPARATE THE FACTS FROM OPINIONS AND GENERALITIES, AND THEN GET RID OF EVERYTHING BUT THE FACTS

Remember that the definition of a fact is something that has been objectively verified, or in the parlance used here, something observed. I recall one story of an observer who, when in the course of a final briefing following an observation, made the subjective statement that "This place is all fouled up." When reminded to stick with the facts, he promptly stated, "This place is all fouled up and that's a fact." Such is not the intent of sticking with the facts.

One final piece of advice on communicating observation results, is,

78. DON'T MIX POSITIVES AND NEGATIVES

Mixing positives and negatives is a technique often used by observers who are unsure of themselves and lack confidence. They seem to believe that if, before telling a manager that he has a problem, they first tell him how good his area looks, and then after describing the problem, they go on to explain how good the workforce is, that the manager will then be less offended and less likely to challenge the existence of the problem. Usually such is not the case, but more importantly, there is a chance that some point will be interpreted as either positive when it should be negative or vice versa. I have seen this happen frequently. Don't leave this to chance. An even more important reason for not mixing positive and negative signals in a report or debrief is that it forces the observer to do his homework and come to the most accurate and well substantiated conclusions. A good example of potential problems from mixing positives and negatives is the following statement extracted from an actual report: "The facility has strong and capable managers, but a management development plan is not in place." What's the point of this statement? If the results are there and the managers are strong and capable, why do they need a plan? If the strong managers were only recently hired from the outside, then the concern of a development plan not being in place may be valid. But if that is the case, it would be much clearer to say that a plan is not in place to develop future managers, and the fact that the current managers are strong is irrelevant. This kind of conflict in messages can be avoided by not mixing positives and negatives.

I'll close this section with what is probably the most important statement in this book:

79. *MAKE SURE YOUR REPORT HAS VALUE*

This includes any report you make as an observer, verbal or written. If it does not have value, protect your reputation and credibility, and save everyone some time -- don't submit it.

Value is an easy thing to check for in a report. Just ask the questions: Does this report tell management something they don't already know, and does it provide enough information to be useful in addressing whatever problems are described in the report? You will likely hear from time to time, some observers defending a weak report that does nothing more than say that everything is OK, by claiming that the report's value lies in the fact that it supports and therefore confirms conclusions already drawn by management. Don't believe it. Recall that every report has a cost. That cost may be the compensation paid the observer, but it may also be in terms of the resources used in supporting the observation -- the time it took workers away from the jobs they are getting paid to do, or the time it takes management away from their duties to even read the report. If the cost of the report is not well offset by the value of the report, the observer has done little more than add unnecessarily to the already large number of challenges that any line organization has.

To reinforce the above point to some managers in my charge, I once insisted that the cost of any observation-related trip be indicated on the top of the first draft of their observation/trip report. I would then assign a subjective grade for value, using the general criteria of whether or not the report told the organization anything they didn't already know. I made a judgment on the relative significance of any new information, considering all of the other challenges to the serviced organization. I subsequently used these grading system results as an input to the individuals' performance appraisals, which in turn, directly affected their pay. Some people hated me for doing this, but over a relatively short period of time, it painted an interesting pattern of who was and was not adding value to my organization's effort. An added benefit of this approach was that subjective "feelings" that I previously had regarding the performance of the observers working for me were now made more objective and allowed for some good opportunities to provide specific and useful feedback to individuals to help in their development.

CHAPTER 8
LEADING A TEAM OF
OBSERVERS

Observations are often charged to teams. These might be formally structured observation teams, but the concept of a team and the principles and techniques referred to here are applicable to other team-oriented oversight activities as well, such as oversight committees or review boards. Leading such a team requires the same leadership skills that leading any endeavor requires. Consequently it is not my intention here to provide the volumes of information that would be needed to describe the various traits, principles, and techniques needed to provide adequate leadership. Instead I will cover only those few points that are unique to leading an oversight team, and which I have found to often be lacking

The most important point to be made in this section is that oversight teams can only be as effective as their leader. In most other endeavors involving a team leader, the team, with sufficient motivation and expertise can produce a reasonable outcome whether or not the leader is even involved. Not so with oversight teams. With oversight teams, the outcome or product flows <u>through</u> the team leader. She not only coaches and motivates the team, but also acts as a sounding board for team members to discuss and refine the problems they have identified; she makes judgments and carries the responsibility for deciding whether or not the problems are valid and objectively based, and whether or not they will add value to the observed organization. She decides which of the problems identified by the team are eventually delivered to the customer. She is accountable for problems that are left unidentified and eventually become self-revealing. She carries the responsibility to not only ensure that the expertise of the team is properly applied in the right areas, but also that all of those areas are adequately covered by the team. She is, in fact, not only the leader of the team but a working member of it also -- if she is doing her job. She needs to not only coordinate, motivate, and in some cases, direct team members, but needs to do it in a way that maximizes their individual contributions by maintaining their ownership and their feeling of accountability. This is true in any leadership position, but even more so in observation space. Most importantly, the leader must achieve a balance by maintaining team ownership and at the same time being <u>directly and intimately</u> involved in the assessment herself. Only with this level of involvement can she attain a level of knowledge sufficient to function as the coach for the team, as the communicator for the team, as the quality check for the team, as the supporter of team issues, as the sounding board for team findings. Failure to achieve this level of involvement is the most frequent shortcoming of observation team leaders. This failure, in turn, is the single largest contributor to team products falling considerably below customer expectations.

The value of and need for an effective team leader is often not recognized when the members of a team are highly experienced and proven observers. Apparently the thought is that such people need no leadership. That is an incorrect conclusion. The need for leadership is even more important when team members are highly experienced and strong individuals themselves. As with many other kinds of teams, the total is considerably more valuable than the sum of the parts. With strong team members but without strong team leadership, synergy of the team will not be achieved and the product will be that much less valuable.

The only way to effectively accomplish this "direct and intimate" involvement is by the team leader putting herself in a frame of mind consistent with the following concept and then operating accordingly:

80. *AN OBSERVATION TEAM LEADER'S ACTIVITIES SHOULD BE GUIDED BY THE PREMISE THAT SHE IS THE ONLY OBSERVER ON THE TEAM*

The leader needs to develop 100 percent ownership of <u>all</u> information collected. Without sharing the concept of AACT 80 openly (and possibly demotivating the team members and diluting their ownership), the leader should work as if other team members are there primarily to be her assistants. She should feel personal ownership and accountability for every problem uncovered by every member of the team. She should not be satisfied with the team's development of any issue that she does not fully understand, that she does not believe is fully supported by facts, and that she does not personally believe to be a problem worthy of the attention of executive management. The level of her comfort must be at a point such that she would feel confident standing before the executive customer and personally debating the merits of the finding. One technique that is effective in achieving this level of involvement is for the team leader to have each member of the team take her into the observed facility, show her any aspect of every problem that observer has identified that is "seeable," and convince her that each problem is a valid one. If the problem is that the healthcare facility is not paying enough attention to building cleanliness, based on conditions in the Operating Room, have the observer take her to the Operating Room where the floor is not meticulously cleaned after each operation. If the problem is that a valve in a production facility was found out of position, have the observer take her into the facility and show her the valve. If the problem is that nurses are not frequently enough turning patients to preclude pressure ulcers or bed sores, have the observer take her to a nursing floor and discreetly show her how patient turning is done, how it is tracked to ensure it is done frequently enough, and any shortfalls that form the basis of the observer's conclusion. This method of "show and tell" can be useful for the observation team members as well. It gives them the opportunity to use the leader as a sounding board and to self-test their understanding and the adequacy of their basis for saying something is a problem.

The concept of the team leader working under the premise that she is the only member of the team not only helps the leader maintain a full sense of ownership for the final product, but also is useful in determining what and how much of the activity the leader should be involved in. If she were really the only observer on the team, she would be involved in everything. Thus, that is the benchmark for involvement. Realistically that may not be possible, but it is the goal for which the leader should strive. If the reader is thinking that this would require an extraordinary amount of additional work by the team leader who already has more than enough to do, I encourage a review of AACT 2 and the role of energy. It should be evident without saying, but just for the completeness of the record, the aforementioned principles cannot be implemented without the team leader's frequent presence in the facility work spaces. A team cannot be effectively lead from an office.

THE CUSTOMER

Every organization and every facility has a myriad of things that can be done better -- "problems," to use our more direct terminology. To unleash a team in such an environment provides a high potential for a scattergun approach, in which some problems will be identified, but not likely those that are most important. The importance of problems in most cases is best determined by the customer. It is the identification of the customer wherein many team leaders fail at the outset. Consequently, to avoid this trap, the team leader needs to,

81. CLEARLY IDENTIFY THE OBSERVATION CUSTOMER AND THE CUSTOMER'S DESIRES UP FRONT

This may seem like an overly obvious step when bringing an observation team into a facility if one assumes that the person in charge of that facility is the customer. Typically this would be an inaccurate assumption. Many observations are initiated by the CEO or other senior level executive, sometimes by one or more members of the Board. The most direct way to determine the customer is to find out who requested the observation, and then confirm that person's identity as the customer with a direct interaction. Often times this is at least one level and sometimes multiple levels above the person directly in charge at the facility to be observed. One can imagine that a person in charge of a facility, if not the real customer, may in fact have an agenda of cosmetically correcting problems to avoid embarrassment, since it is likely that this person is the one who caused or at least contributed to any problems that exist.

FOCUSING

Once the customer is identified, a short discussion with him will allow determination of the purpose of the observation. At this point, the leader should,

82. *DEVELOP A CLEAR, CONCISE, AND HIGH LEVEL OBJECTIVE FOR THE OBSERVATION*

Again, many team leaders take for granted that the objective is obvious -- to identify problems. They then skip this important step. However, an objective with a finer point on it will be useful in focusing the team and will also help to ensure the team, in addition to identifying problems, is achieving what the customer desires. Examples of objectives that I have used include:

- Determine why the organization's performance has plateaued or declined.

- Identify any significant improvement needs that are not already identified and that do not have corrective actions already underway.

- Determine if, in the team's opinion, the facility is working on the right things with the right priorities

The customer should be in agreement with the objective, but the objective should be developed by the team. Involving the team in defining the objective, while still considering the desires of the customer, will help to build the team's ownership of the entire evolution.

Team leaders have a natural tendency to want things to move along smoothly and rapidly, and that is good. The one area that is most likely to present obstacles to this smooth running is that of logistics, which include travel, housing, food arrangements, meeting locations, and so on. These last two statements, taken together lead to the logical conclusion that the team leader should be directly involved in the logistics. That would be a mistake. As important as logistics are, they have least of all to do with providing the substance needed in the final report that will be the gauge of quality and value in the final product provided to the customer. Unfortunately, resolving logistics and other ancillary problems is also the area that can cause the greatest loss of observation time. Ancillaries like logistics are critical to the success of the team; however, they should not be allowed to dilute the team leader's relentless drive for value in the final product. Consequently, delegation of logistics -- to a highly competent person -- is essential.

PROVIDING DIRECTION

Personnel selected for oversight teams are typically high caliber people with exceptional expertise and unquestionable motivation. That said, for such a group to operate as a single entity, and to operate with a high degree of effectiveness, all must march in the same direction. Consequently, the leader needs to

83. SET CLEAR EXPECTATIONS -- PREFERABLY IN WRITING

Written expectations allow the more conscientious observers to have them at their finger tips for reference and reinforcement. Again, setting clear direction is an important part of any leader's role; however, in the world of observations, specific direction becomes even more important. The more experienced the team members, and the more capable they are of operating independently, the more important this specific direction becomes. Without it the "team" becomes just a bunch of people. With the direction, synergy comes into play and adds to the value. These expectations should include, in addition to achievement of the objective discussed above, what else the team leader expects in terms of expected level of preparation, type and quality of written products and when these products are to be ready, times for any key activities such as team meetings, expected preparation for and conduct expected in team meetings, expected contributions to general management areas such as accountability and alignment, and finally, expected working hours and backshift coverage. The latter provides an opportunity to set the highest expectations for the degree of effort expected of team members.

The team leader, in keeping with AACT 79 [MAKE SURE YOUR REPORT HAS VALUE] should continuously be alert for opportunities to apply the synergistic capabilities of the team in the gathering of information. Expectations as well should guide the team members to look for similar opportunities. Having all team members ask the same question to a wide range of people can provide valuable insight. For example, a good team-wide question to ask of those observed is, What message do you most frequently hear from management? Responses to this question from a range of employees might reveal that the executive who says that patient safety is the highest priority, may, inadvertently or otherwise, be sending his employees a message that cost rather than safety is the first thing to consider. Another team question that can provide valuable insight can be applied if there are peers from other organizations on the team. Have the peers ask or take note of how frequently, and by what level of staff at the facility being observed, they are asked about their experiences and how things are done at their facility. A later tally of the amount of interest shown by the organization being observed gives good insight to whether or not that organization is isolated from and uninterested in the performance of their peers, and is thus on the road to complacency.

In summary, the team leader should draw on that fundamental attribute of energy included in AACT 2 [EXPERIENCE, EXPOSURE, AND ENERGY ARE THE REQUISITE ATTRIBUTES OF A GOOD OBSERVER] and lead by exampleship as well as leadership, the exercise of which both contribute to the value of a team.

EPILOGUE

Eighty-three AACTs are discussed in this book. The reader may find that number unusual and wonder about its genesis. The number has no special significance. There are many more concepts and techniques in the world of observation than those discussed here. Some I'm sure are even yet to be discovered or applied. I have resisted the temptation to use the book-marketing advantage of rounding out the number to an even 100, and instead have exerted my best effort to provide only value. To achieve that end I have shared those concepts and techniques that have best proved their value to me over almost five decades. The number turns out to be eighty-three. You, as an observer, will develop or discover your own AACTs as your experience in this important activity broadens. Make note of these AACTs and share them with your peers and with those who will follow in the footprints you leave as you walk in your oversight role. By doing so, you will be contributing to improved performance through use of the most effective implement in the oversight tool chest -- the observant eye.

APPENDIX 1
EXPECTATIONS FOR
CORPORATE OVERSIGHT OF
TRAINING

The Corporate Training Organization is expected to remain apprised of the state and effectiveness of training at the Operating Facilities. The purpose of this oversight follows:

1. To identify areas where corporate support can be provided to help solve facility problems.
2. To provide an input to senior management regarding the health of the training programs.
3. To ensure escalation of important issues to an appropriate level of management.

Methods for performing this oversight will include the following:

1. Visits to the facilities
2. Observations of training and site activities
3. Discussions with Line and Training personnel
4. Review of performance data such as training

> feedback, attendance statistics, and facility performance data

5. Participation in training related meetings at the facility

6. Support of assessments and audits, either as requested or proactively initiated by corporate management

Oversight activities are to identify strengths and weaknesses that, as a minimum, address the following:

1. Strengths that can be used at our other facilities

2. Issues that could threaten the accreditation or certification of training programs, particularly those that the corporate office can be helpful in resolving

3. Lack of support of the standardization of training programs across the facilities

4. Initiatives started by the corporate office that are beyond baseline staff loading and that may impact the application of resources to higher priority activities

5. Shortfalls in complying with regulatory required training

6. Lack of awareness by the facility training staff of actions needed to address the operating experience of our other facilities

7. Effectiveness of the use and maintenance of simulators

8. Effectiveness of corrective actions taken to address known training problems

APPENDIX 2
TRAINING PRINCIPLES

---

1   Corporate Training exists only to provide oversight and support to the operating facilities.

2. Training improvements are driven by line management.

3. The only valid reason for any training activity is to provide well-trained and qualified people.

4. Training is important facility work. As such, it is scheduled, executed, and monitored like any other important work.

5. No one is to be more critical of facility training activities and performance than the people operating that facility.

6. The line owns training.

7   Training owns performance.

8.   Each facility is aware of training strengths and weaknesses at other facilities and acts on that knowledge to improve.

9.   Training programs and practices are standardized between facilities to achieve economies of scale.

10.   Training activities and conditions set the example for the high standards expected in all areas of performance.

APPENDIX 3
OBSERVABLE BEHAVIORS
OF LINE OWNERSHIP OF
TRAINING

---

1. Line managers are held accountable for the training and qualification of the employees reporting to them. This accountability should be apparent in the directions provided to managers by senior managers, perceptions of the line managers, entries in performance appraisals, and disciplinary measures, if warranted.

2. Line managers can speak knowledgeably of how training was developed and the basis for any training.

3. Line managers approve technical training content as indicated by signatures on lesson plans or training guides.

4. Line managers ensure that training reinforces human performance expectations such as use of error reduction techniques.

5.   Management expectations for ownership of training are defined, promulgated, and understood.

6.   Senior management communicates regularly, using forums such as newsletters and all employees meetings, that training plays a key role in improving site performance.

7.   A clear policy regarding training attendance is implemented. It includes strong action for non-adherence.

8.   Line managers insist on a high degree of adherence to the training schedule.

9.   Line managers lead those groups set up to monitor and improve training, such as Training Councils or Training Advisory Committees.

10. Training is at authorized staffing or actions are underway to achieve that staffing.

11. Final qualification of personnel is approved by line management.

12. Qualification is monitored to ensure timely completion.

13. Line managers determine who attends training.

14. Senior management periodically meets with training management to communicate expectations and resolve training problems.

15. Subject Matter Experts are used to enhance training.

16. Training in all settings is frequently monitored (typically two observations per month for each individual required to monitor) and senior management ensures the monitoring covers all areas and involves all appropriate personnel. This monitoring results in critical feedback that is used to revise training.

17. Detailed action plans are in place to address key training problems, and line manager's names are evident in the assignments.

18. Line managers provide feedback to the training organization on the effectiveness of training based on worker feedback and performance.

19. Training performance indicators are monitored by line management.

20. First-line supervisors attend continuing training with their workers.

21. Senior management periodically communicates with the Trainers to relay expectations and foster the importance and value of training.

APPENDIX 4
SUMMARY OF ACCTS

---

1.   THINK PERFORMANCE-BASED

2.   EXPERIENCE, EXPOSURE, AND ENERGY ARE THE REQUISITE ATTRIBUTES OF A GOOD OBSERVER

3.   THERE ARE ALWAYS PROBLEMS OUT THERE

4.   DON'T BE AN INDUSTRIAL TOURIST

5.   YOU WON'T FIND WHAT YOU AREN'T LOOKING FOR

6.   PROBLEMS COME IN EITHER OF TWO FORMS -- THINGS THAT ARE DONE INCORRECTLY, AND THINGS THAT ARE NOT DONE BUT SHOULD BE. THE LATTER ARE MORE FREQUENTLY OVERLOOKED

7. **WRONG IS ANYTHING THAT ISN'T AS GOOD AS IT CAN BE**

8. **DIFFERENT IS NOT WRONG**

9. **SO WHAT?**

10. **LET NO ONE BE MORE CRITICAL OF YOU THAN YOU**

11. **YOU HAVE TO BE WILLING TO CALL YOUR BABY UGLY**

12. **IGNORE THE GRAY INFORMATION**

13. **FOCUS ON IMPLEMENTATION**

14. **APPLY Y CUBED**

15. **PULL THE STRING**

16. **GO SEE FOR YOURSELF**

17. **USE 3X5 CARDS**

18. **GET IN THE TRENCHES**

19. **LOOK FOR "MANAGEMENT TRACKS"**

20. **CONTINUALLY FORM HYPOTHESES AND THEN PROVE OR DISPROVE THEM**

21. **WRITE DOWN EVERYTHING**

22. **STIR THE TEA LEAVES**

34. IF YOU WANT TO UNDERSTAND WHAT'S GOING ON IN AN ORGANIZATION, WATCH THE PEOPLE. CONVERSELY, IF YOU DON'T WATCH THE PEOPLE, YOU WON'T KNOW WHAT'S REALLY GOING ON IN AN ORGANIZATION

35. TOUR GUIDES PROVIDE AN ADDED OPPORTUNITY

36. AS MEETINGS GO, SO GOES THE ORGANIZATION

37. TRAINING IS A MICROCOSM OF AN ORGANIZATION

38. ORGANIZATIONS OFTEN DO TOO MUCH TRAINING -- AND ON THE WRONG THINGS

39. TRAINING PROBLEMS FORESHADOW ORGANIZATIONAL PROBLEMS

40. THE PIVOTAL QUESTION REGARDING ANY SELF-ASSESSMENT EFFORT IS NOT, WHAT IS THE QUALITY OF SELF-ASSESSMENT, BUT RATHER, DO THE MANAGERS KNOW WHAT'S GOING ON

41. DON'T MINE THE SELF-ASSESSMENT DATA

42 DON'T FORGET TO WATCH THE WATCHERS

43. IF YOU CONTINUE TO DIG IN THE SAME HOLE, DON'T BE SURPRISED TO FIND THE SAME DIRT

44. OBSERVING HOW WELL AN ORGANIZATION IDENTIFIES, IMPLEMENTS, AND FOLLOWS UP ON CORRECTIVE ACTION IS LIKE TAKING THE PULSE OF THAT ORGANIZATION TO DETERMINE ONE OF ITS VITAL SIGNS

45. DIG INTO CORRECTIVE ACTIONS, BUT DON'T REPACKAGE PROBLEMS AND CALL THEM YOUR FINDINGS

46. BEWARE OF THE DOWNSIDES OF ROOT CAUSE ANALYSIS

47. DON'T TRY TO SOLVE WORLD HUNGER

48. LOOK FOR THE LINE TO BE KEPT RESPONSIBLE -- AND ACCOUNTABLE -- FOR DEFINING CORRECTIVE ACTIONS AND THEIR PRIORITIES

49. EFFECTIVE CORRECTIVE ACTION EFFORTS WILL ONLY FLOURISH IN A FOSTERING ENVIRONMENT

50. DON'T WASTE TIME LOOKING AT RESPONSES TO A PROBLEM UNLESS THAT PROBLEM IS FIRST VERIFIED TO STILL EXIST

51. TAKING TOO MANY CORRECTIVE ACTIONS IS QUICKSAND IN THE MANAGEMENT JUNGLE

52. LOOK FOR "RESULTS PLANS" NOT ACTION PLANS

53. A BIG PLAN ISN'T NECESSARILY A GOOD PLAN

54. "DONE" REALLY MEANS DONE, THAT IS, DONE-DONE

55. THE VALUE OF A USED CAR DEPENDS ON THE CONDITION OF THE CAR, NOT THE INTENTIONS OF THE OWNER

56. IT TAKES MANAGEMENT ALIGNMENT TO MOVE AN ORGANIZATION IN A CONSISTENT DIRECTION

57. ANY ORGANIZATION WILL WORK

58. CONSISTENT ADHERENCE TO EXPECTATIONS IS A HALLMARK OF A TOP PERFORMING ORGANIZATION

59. NOT PAYING ATTENTION TO PEOPLE PERFORMANCE IS NOT PAYING ATTENTION TO PERFORMANCE

60. BE SENSITIVE TO WHAT THOSE IN CHARGE ARE SUPPOSED TO DO AND OBSERVE THEM DOING IT

61. ACCOUNTABILITY IS THE SIGN OF A HEALTHY ORGANIZATION

61a. BE SKEPTICAL OF THE CONCLUSION THAT "THINGS ARE ALL SCREWED UP BUT EVERYBODY IS DOING A GREAT JOB"

61b. BE ALERT FOR HAPPY TALK--PARTICULARLY IN MEETINGS

62. COMPLACENCY IS MOST EVIDENT IN THE LACK OF LEARNING FROM OTHERS

63. BELIEVE YOUR WORST INDICATION

64. BEWARE OF THE NEW GUY TELLING YOU EVERYTHING IS BROKEN

65. IF YOU DON'T HAVE A PERFORMANCE PROBLEM, YOU DON'T HAVE A MANAGEMENT PROBLEM

66. A PROBLEM MATRIX IS A SELF-PORTRAIT OF THE EFFECTIVENESS OF THE MANAGEMENT TEAM

67. OBSERVERS PROVIDE A MIRROR FOR MANAGERS

68. PAY ATTENTION TO THE GUT FEELINGS OF EXPERIENCED PEOPLE

69. YOU CAN'T HAVE A FOCUS ON GOOD OPERATION WITHOUT HAVING A FOCUS ON SAFETY

70. CORPORATE EXISTS FOR A PRIMARY REASON -- TO PROVIDE SUPPORT AND OVERSIGHT OF THE OPERATING FACILITIES

71. AN EXAMPLE IS WORTH A THOUSAND WORDS

72. MAKE NOTE OF POSITIVES

73. **PRIORITIZE YOUR KEY POINTS AND KEEP THEM TO A FEW**

74. **THE MISSION OF AN OBSERVER IS NOT ONLY TO FIND PROBLEMS, IT IS TO PRECIPITATE POSITIVE CHANGE**

75. **TELL A COMPELLING STORY**

76. **IF YOU CAN'T DESCRIBE A PROBLEM IN ONE OR TWO SIMPLE SENTENCES, YOU DON'T UNDERSTAND THE PROBLEM**

77. **SEPARATE THE FACTS FROM OPINIONS AND GENERALITIES, AND THEN GET RID OF EVERYTHING BUT THE FACTS**

78. **DON'T MIX POSITIVES AND NEGATIVES**

79. **MAKE SURE YOUR REPORT HAS VALUE**

80. **AN OBSERVATION TEAM LEADER'S ACTIVITIES SHOULD BE GUIDED BY THE PREMISE THAT SHE IS THE ONLY OBSERVER ON THE TEAM**

81. **CLEARLY IDENTIFY THE OBSERVATION CUSTOMER AND THE CUTOMER'S DESIRES UP FRONT**

82. **DEVELOP A CLEAR, CONCISE, AND HIGH LEVEL OBJECTIVE FOR THE OBSERVATION**

83. **SET CLEAR EXPECTATIONS -- PREFERABLY IN WRITING**

Made in the USA
Lexington, KY
12 June 2019